OUT OF BOUNDS

What Happened to the Yuba County Five?

Drew Hurst Beeson

Fort Necessity Press

CONTENTS

DISCLAIMER

The assumptions, interpretations, opinions, ideas, and analyses expressed in this book are those of the author and do not reflect the position of any other person or organization. The views expressed are subject to revision as new information comes to light.

This book is a work of non-fiction. Some parts have been dramatized in order to provide the reader with an authentic feel for the time period and a broader context surrounding pivotal events.

.

DEDICATION

This book is dedicated to the lasting memories of Jack "Doc" Madruga, Theodore "Ted" Weiher, Jack "Jackie" Huett, William "Bill" Sterling, and Gary Mathias.

May the surviving loved ones of these beloved "Boys" someday find closure to this tragedy that has burdened them for far too long.

A special thank you to the following people for making this book possible: The Jackie Huett Family, Tammie Mathias Phillips, George Madruga, and Cathy Madruga Roberts.

An honest man here lies at rest,
The friend of man, the friend of truth,
The friend of age, and guide of youth:
Few hearts like his, with virtue warm'd,
Few heads with knowledge so inform'd;
If there's another world, he lives in bliss;
If there is none, he made the best of this.

-Robert Burns

"*It has occurred to me, brother, that wisdom may not be the end of everything. Goodness and kindness are, perhaps, beyond wisdom. It is possible that the ultimate is gaiety and music and a dance of joy.*"

- Quote from the Marysville High School 1971 Yearbook

Marysville High School, circa 1971

FOREWORD

This case is bizarre as hell.

- Yuba County Undersheriff Jack Beecham

February 1978

T he Yuba County Undersheriff simply could not think of a better choice of words than "bizarre as hell" to describe how five grown men, who had attended a basketball game an hour's drive from their homes on a Friday night, simply never made it back to their families. For many months after their disappearance, not even a trace of their whereabouts was found despite frantic and thorough searching.

Adding to the intrigue of this classic American missing persons case is that four of the missing men had some form of cognitive disability. The fifth man was a diagnosed schizophrenic who had a history of violent outbursts, arrests, and drug use. According to their families, "the Boys," as they were affectionately called, would not just disappear. Not telling anyone where they were going was highly unusual, especially in light of the fact that all five of the Boys were set to play in a Special Olympics basketball tournament regional playoff game the next day, something that each of them had been looking forward to for months.

In this book, I have made a heartfelt effort to piece together the known facts of this case, many of which have been misreported; present all known theories of what may have caused the Boys to disappear; and examine the merits of these theories. This case raises many more questions than it answers, which is one reason why it is one of the most fascinating mysteries in American history. This case is known as "The Yuba County Five" as the Boys came from the Yuba County, California towns of Yuba City,

Marysville, Linda, and Olivehurst.

This book is the most comprehensive account to date of this occurrence and will present all known facts, theories, and speculations about this case. The story of the Yuba County Five is one of mystery, intrigue, bewilderment, and most of all, tragedy and sadness. For the families of these young men, the sense of heartbreak and loss is just as strong today as it was over forty years ago.

PROLOGUE

1962

Ida Mathias Klopf tried to smooth out her son's wrinkled clip-on tie as she shooshed him out the door. It was a hopeless endeavor. She knew that Gary must have pulled out that tie from the pile of clothes in the corner of his closet. "How is it possible for one kid to dirty so many clothes?" she thought. "Well, at least the rest of his suit looks all right."

"Gary, stop dragging your feet. We are not gonna be late for church again, and we need to stop real quick at the store first to get a card for the pastor!" she said as she walked toward the blue '58 Dodge station wagon in which her two daughters were waiting, probably not very patiently.

In the ten years since Gary had been born, Ida had learned to be patient. It seemed to take forever for the family to get ready to go anywhere. She thought of her daughters, Sharon and Tammie. They were usually ready on time. But Gary? Gary was different. Different in so many ways.

Ida opened the driver's side door. "Ready to go, girls," she said both forcefully and apologetically at the same time, hoping that neither (or both) of her daughters would now have to run back into the house and go to the bathroom.

"Gary couldn't find a tie that didn't have a stain on it," she said, as if an explanation were necessary, and slid into the driver's seat while Gary walked over to the passenger side, opened the door and said, "Out," to Tammie who was sitting there. For a moment, Tammie thought of appealing to her mother, but instead she just sighed, got up, opened the back door, and sat down. Satisfied with himself, Gary plopped into the front seat and smiled. Gary never sat in the back seat – one of the privileges of being an older brother.

With everyone seated, Ida started the car, and they headed for the Food Faire, one of the few stores open on Sunday morning. It was a short drive without much traffic, and the family rode together silently, each trying to fully wake up and become less uncomfortable in their church clothes.

Gary couldn't wait for the ride to be over. It wasn't as if he really looked forward to church; he just wanted to get out of the car. Bored, he fiddled with the door handle, listening to the sound it made as his fingers slid back and forth on it. Then an idea struck him – why wait? And as his mother eased the car into a right turn approaching the back entrance to the Food Faire, Gary opened the car door and tumbled out of the moving vehicle and into the street.

It took but an instant for his sisters to start screaming and for his mother to slam on the brakes and run into the street to see her son lying on the pavement, his head in a pool of blood. Ida's first instinct was to panic, but, thankfully, a man walking nearby had seen what had happened and helped Ida get Gary back into the car. She then sped to the hospital in Yuba City.

Gary was in bad shape. When he arrived at the ER, they rushed him back and put him in a private room. After a few hours, Gary regained consciousness. As he came to, he said in a groggy voice, "What happened? Why are the lights out?"

"Gary, Gary. The lights are not out," his mother said as she put her hand on his shoulder, trying to ease his agitation.

Gary could hear his mother's voice, but he couldn't see her. "Mom, I can't see!" he screamed in horror as he tried to sit up in his hospital bed. He couldn't see, and his head hurt worse than it ever had. His whole body hurt worse than it ever had.

"Gary, Gary," his mom continued to try to soothe him. "I am going to ring for the doctor," she said as she pushed the call button at the side of Gary's bed. In a minute, a nurse rushed into Gary's room, glanced around, and went for a doctor, who returned with her a few minutes later.

"Gary, you've had a serious head injury. Your sight will come back in a few days as the swelling goes down and your brain heals. You need a lot of rest," the doctor explained as the nurse injected morphine into Gary's IV. "Make sure he rests," the doctor said as he left the room. "You should be able to go home in a few days."

Gary relaxed as the morphine kicked in, and he quickly fell asleep. Exhausted, Ida went to a vending machine, got a cup of coffee with extra sugar, and used a pay phone to call her mother and tell her that Gary was now awake and would be fine. Then she went back to Gary's room, pulled a chair close to his bed and stared at him while he slept, wondering why Gary would do such a thing. Why would he open the car door while the car was moving? Why?

About four days later, Gary started to see light. He could make out figures, but his vision was very blurry. Slowly his vision came back, but it never came back fully, and he was forced to wear extremely thick glasses, which he hated.

"I have to wear these? I will look like a goofball, Mom!" Gary lamented at his first eyeglasses fitting.

Gary had to wear his coke-bottle glasses for years, but a couple of weeks before he went missing, he had gotten contact lenses, which he liked to wear when he was playing basketball because there were no frames to interfere with his field of vision or to slide down his nose.

Fast Forward to June 1977

Gateway Projects Facilities
Yuba City, California

The fifteen years that followed Gary's falling-out-of-the-car incident were good and bad for Gary: sports successes, high school graduation, military service, psychological issues, legal problems, and substance abuse. The last of these led Gary to the drug counseling offices of the Gateway Projects in Yuba City, California. Although Gateway generally focused on intellectually challenged individuals, it also served as a catch-all for troubled young men.

It was after a drug counseling appointment at Gateway that Gary would meet the four men with whom he would be forever linked. As Gary walked into Gateway's reception area, 10 minutes late for his weekly 3:00 appointment with Don, he nodded to Kelly, who was busy typing away at something at the front desk. She looked up at him and smiled as he signed his name on the patient log-in sheet. Gary smiled back at her and was glad that he was wearing his lucky Rolling Stones World Tour '75 tee shirt. He was hoping that she would comment on his shirt and maybe they could get a conversation going, and he stood at the reception desk a bit longer than was necessary, taking off his glasses and wiping them wit the hem of his shirt, looking at her and waiting for her to say something.

All she said was, "Don will be with you shortly."

And Gary's chest, clad in yellow with a giant bird of prey emblazoned across it, sank a little, and he walked away from the desk, found the cleanest-looking chair, and sat down on it.

He had only been sitting for about a minute when he was called back. Gary effortlessly eased himself out of the chair and sauntered nonchalantly to Don's office, appearing to have not a care in the world. At least that was the impression he was trying to make. Nonchalant. Not a care in the world. Seen it all. Done it all. Jaded. *Nonchalant*. It takes a lot of effort to appear as if you don't care, and Gary really did care, but he didn't want anyone to know it.

Don, Gary's substance abuse counselor, really did care, too. Don was a throwback, a former addict from the '60s era, who had been clean for 8 years but had never lost the king hair, sideburns, and hippie clothes.

Don was holding Gary's chart as Gary walked into his office, and he motioned for Gary to sit down.

"You have been doing great, Gary," Don said to him. "I think this doctor you are going to now has finally got you on the right combination of psych meds. Just keep fighting the temptation to slip back into old habits. You know - you can't mix those psych meds with the street stuff, Gary. I don't want to come off like a broken record, man, but you know what happened last time. I know you have been doing well lately, but I know how those guys can be around Olivehurst. Temptation is everywhere."

Gary pulled his chair closer to Don and proceeded to put his feet on the counselor's desk. *Nonchalant*. Once he had made himself comfortable, he looked directly at Don and responded, "Temptation *is* everywhere. All the time, man."

Don resisted the temptation to tell Gary not to put his feet on the desk and said instead, "One of the best ways to avoid temptation is to keep yourself busy. Remember, idle hands are the devil's workshop. What have you been doing with yourself lately, besides working?"

Gary looked down and muttered that he really wasn't doing much. He had been seeing this girl that he had dated in high school, but he didn't even get to see her all that much.

"I guess I lead a pretty boring life now, just an old man, I guess,"

Gary joked and looked up at Don.

Don met Gary's gaze. "I got you this little notepad," Don said as he handed a small reporter's spiral notebook across the desk to Gary.

Gary turned the notebook over in his hand and asked, "What in hell am I supposed to do with this?"

He put the notepad in his left hand and pretended to write on it with the index finger of his right hand.

"Can I take your order, sir?" Gary said sarcastically.

Don smiled. "No, Gary. Here's what I want you to do, man. Write little notes to yourself, notes of encouragement to help you get through the day, to help you stay on the wagon. You know, the power of positive thinking and all that. Like *The Little Engine that Could*."

Don caught his breath for a second and continued, "Let's start off with one now. How about you write down, *I believe in me*, ok?"

Gary picked out a pen from the pencil holder on the desk and proceeded to write. After he had finished, he looked up at Don and said, reading from page, "I will be the next Mick Jagger." Then he closed the cover of the little notepad with a flourish and stated, "First note of encouragement written."

Don laughed and said, "Well, it's a start. But seriously, writing notes to yourself is a time-tested way of helping you stay on track. Working with other people helps, too, you know, helps to take you out of your own head for a while. And with that in mind, I was thinking about something. I remember you used to play football at Marysville High, right?"

"'Yeah, I played my sophomore and junior years. I was pretty good."

"What about basketball?" Don queried.

"Yeah," Gary replied. I played some basketball, too."

"Good. I need someone who knows a little about basketball to help out with teaching some of the guys here who want to play on our Special Olympics team," Don said enthusiastically. "One of the guys is a really good player, but he can't seem to show his buddies how it's done. They are all a little slow upstairs, if you know what I mean, but they are great guys and have a lot of heart. What do you say?"

Gary thought for a moment. He really did miss playing basketball. Not just shooting baskets in the driveway but playing on a team. A basketball team. Yeah, he missed that. "Sure. I'll do it," he said. "When do I start?"

Don stood up. "How about now? Let's go the gym. They should all be there."

"All right," Gary said and followed Don out the door, across the courtyard, and into an adjoining building.

The men could hear the sounds of basketballs being dribbled on a wooden floor and basketballs hitting backboards as they walked down the hallway toward two sets of double doors. The sounds filled Gary with a sense of belonging, like he was coming home. The sounds grew louder as Don pushed open one of the double doors with Gary following closely behind him. It took a moment for Gary's eyes to adjust to the bright lights of the court, and both men stood there in front of the doorway until the basketball players realized that Gary and Don were watching them, just out of bounds.

At that point, the players stopped their practice, and one of them, Ted Weiher, began waving excitedly, shouting, "Hi Gary!"

Gary looked at Ted and called back, "Hi Ted," as Ted Weiher began walking toward Gary and Don.

Gary turned to Don, "Ted lives just down the street from me."

Ted was obviously happy to see someone from his neighborhood, and with Ted in tow, Don began to introduce Gary to everyone else.

Bill Sterling smiled at Gary and said, "Hello," in his bashful, gentle manner.

Jackie Huett was glad to have a new friend and made an unusual happy, laughing sound upon meeting Gary. Gary was kind of taken aback by this, but he tried not to let it show.

"Don't worry about Jackie, Gary," Ted explained. "He wants to learn to play. Me, too." He paused for a second and then added, "Doc plays good."

Ted pointed and waved to Jack "Doc" Madruga, who was sitting on the bleachers, looking on but saying nothing. Doc nodded politely when Gary was introduced to him, but he was not fond of change, especially when the change would affect one of the things he loved – his basketball team, The Gateway Gators.

CHAPTER 1: "THE BOYS"

Excitement was most certainly in the cool air late on the Friday afternoon of February 24, 1978, in the working-class town of Marysville, California (population just over 10,000). Five friends, affectionately called the Boys by family and practically everyone who knew them, were getting ready to attend a basketball game at California State University – Chico, roughly a 50-minute drive due north of Marysville. The Boys were thrilled to see their favorite team, the UC Davis Aggies, take on the Chico State Wildcats. They practically hero-worshiped the UC Davis players.

Although they were called the Boys, they all were men, ranging in age from 24 to 32 years. Four of them had some form of learning/cognitive disability that made their demeanor and behavior more like that of younger-aged boys; thus, the nickname, which was used lovingly. It has been reported that three of the Boys were diagnosed as "mentally retarded" (a term that was not pejorative in the 1970s). The families of the Boys have stated that the Boys were indeed slightly intellectually impaired but were capable of "functioning normally in public and in social situations." (Gorney, 5 'Boys' Who Never Come Back, *The Washington Post*, July 6, 1978)

The Boys consisted of Ted Weiher, Bill Sterling, Jackie Huett, Jack Madruga, and Gary Mathias. They met at the Gateway Projects, located at a vocational rehabilitation center in Yuba City. The Gateway Projects Program was formed in January 1971 and was "designed to prepare handicapped and disadvantaged persons for competitive employment." (*Marysville Appeal Democrat*, Marysville, CA, November 18, 1971, page 9) The program was open to a wide array of people with various conditions, including cerebral palsy, cognitive disability, mental illness, emotional issues, epilepsy, and multiple sclerosis.

The Gateway Projects sponsored a basketball team called The Gateway Gators, on which all the Boys played. Adding to the excitement of Friday night, February 24, was the Boys' knowledge that on the following day, they would be playing in a Special

Olympics basketball tournament district playoff round, held at Sierra College in nearby Rockling, California. The Boys, with the exception of Gary Mathias, had gone to Sacramento the previous Thursday to practice basketball for their upcoming game.

The winning team of the playoff round was to be given an all-expenses-paid trip to Los Angeles, where they would get to meet *All in the Family* T.V. show actress Sally Struthers. According to Jack's mother Melba Madruga, Jack had gotten Sally Struthers' autograph when he was part of a Special Olympics team that had made the playoffs the prior year.

THE GATEWAY GATORS. composed of Hub area Gateway clients, will be uniformed when they compete in athletic events or the handicapped.

That's the word from Gateway. Tee shirts have been purchased with donations from the Olivehurst Lions Club, the John A. Sutter branch of the Business and Professional Women, the Tierra Buena Women's Club, the Yuba - Sutter High Twelve, the Early Risers and the Yuba City Kiwanis Club.

The tee shirts all carry the Gateway Gators' emblem.

Marysville Appeal Democrat, Marysville, California, US
January 29, 1977, Page 18

In addition to their love of basketball, the Boys also enjoyed bowling together every Saturday in Yuba City and sometimes on their trips to Sacramento. The Boys were happy in their own world.

HUETT   STERLING   MADRUGA   WEIHER   MATHIAS

Sacramento Bee, March 28, 1978

TED WEIHER

Ted Weiher
Marysville High School yearbook photo, 1964

Theodore "Ted" Weiher, age 32, was the perfect example of a boy trapped in man's body. Like all the Boys, Ted lived at home with his parents. He was six feet tall and 200 pounds with curly hair and brown eyes. It was said that Ted had a "mind like a child." His family often called him Teddy Bear due to his innocent disposition.

Ted was described as "beer-bellied" with a happy-go-lucky and friendly personality that endeared him to family and friends. As an adult, Ted would often wave excitedly at strangers and would become upset for hours if they did not wave back at him, believing that he had done something wrong. (Gorney, 5 'Boys' Who Never Come Back, *The Washington Post*, July 6, 1978)

Ted was described by one of his brothers as "lacking common sense." Ted's brother told a story about a time that their family home caught on fire, and he was forced to carry Ted out of the house because Ted refused to leave his bed since he had to get up early and go to work the next day. Ted's family also told of an incident during which Ted bought $100 worth of pencils for no particular reason. (Gorney, 5 'Boys' Who Never Come Back, *The Washington Post,* July 6, 1978)

Ted briefly held a job working as a clerk at a local snack bar, but his parents made him quit the job because they feared it would cause too much stress for him. He would later do work at the Gateway Projects facility, repairing damaged cable for the Pacific Gas and Electric Company, with which Gateway contracted.

"Ted was a very loving person," his mother said the day after he was buried. "He loved life, and he loved people." Ted was a graduate of Marysville High School, where he set a record for throwing the softball for distance. (*The Sacramento Bee*, June 14, 1978.)

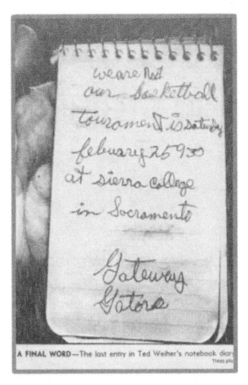

A FINAL WORD—The last entry in Ted Weiher's notebook diary

Ted asked his mom to wash his brand new white high-topped sneakers for the Special Olympics basketball tournament. He had scuffed them during practice and wanted them to look perfect.

BILL STERLING

William "Bill" Sterling
Placer High School - Senior Yearbook photo

William "Bill" Sterling, age 29, enjoyed spending time with his best friend Jack Madruga. Like Ted Weiher, Bill was said to "have a mind like a child." (*The Sacramento Bee*, June 14, 1978) Ted really enjoyed calling Bill on the telephone to read him funny-sounding names from the newspaper.

Faith was at the center of Bill's life, and he would often visit people in mental hospitals and read the Bible and other religious texts to them.

Bill Sterling worked at Sunsweet Growers, a dried fruit company, after his friend Jack Madruga had gotten him a job there as a dishwasher. Sterling was not at Sunsweet for long because he had difficulty operating the new dishwashing equipment that the company installed shortly after he had started there. Sterling acquired another dishwashing job at Beale Air Force Base, but his mother made him quit when she found out that the men at the base would get Sterling drunk and steal his money.

Bill lived at home with his parents, and with the exception of going to church, playing basketball, going to the library, and attending the Gateway Projects, he rarely left his house. He was 5'10" and 160 pounds with black hair and blue eyes.

He loved to read and spent a lot of time at the library "doing research about mentally handicapped people" according to his sisters Deanna and Debbie, who are identical twins. He also regularly attended Marysville Community Church. (*The Sacramento Bee*, June 14, 1878) Bill was a graduate of Placer High School in nearby Auburn, California.

Bill considered Jack Madruga to be his best friend, but he was also close friends with Ted Weiher, whom he had known for about eight years before they went missing.

JACK MADRUGA

Jack Madruga
Marysville High School Senior Photo 1965

Doc [Jack's nickname] was my standby.
- Jack Madruga's mother

J ack Madruga, age 30 at the time of his disappearance, was born and raised in Yuba County. Jack was an Army veteran and had served in Vietnam in 1968. Jack lived with his mother Melba Gail Madruga in a trailer home in the Mulberry Mobile Estates Park in Linda, California, just outside of Marysville. Jack was 5'10," and 190 pounds with brown hair and hazel eyes.

Jack Madruga, nicknamed "Doc" by his family because he was fond of saying *What's up, Doc?*, loved playing sports and was also a good student.

Doc's prized possession was his 1969 Mercury Montego. He would never allow anyone but himself to drive it. Doc bought his beloved Montego by using his Army allotment and some money he had earned from working. As he and Gary were the only two Boys who had driver's licenses, Jack was almost always the driver for the group because Gary did not own a car.

Jack, according to his mother, was never diagnosed as "mentally retarded" but was generally thought of as "slow." According to his family, Jack was able to manage his own finances. (*Marysville Appeal Democrat*, March 2, 1978)

According to Jack's nephew George Madruga, Jack "was an intelligent and sensitive man. Just extremely shy in social situations." George also told me, "Jack's favorite TV show was *I Love Lucy*. He liked to laugh at all the comedy shows of the time. He also enjoyed game shows, and we would play board games for hours." Jack also liked to listen to Motown music. His favorite group was Diana Ross and The Supremes. As George Madruga puts it, "He loved the music he could dance to."

Jack had been laid off as a busboy and dishwasher from the dried fruit company, Sunsweet Growers, not long before he went missing. He was a graduate of Marysville High School and attended Yuba College.

JACKIE HUETT

Jackie Huett – AP Photo

J ack "Jackie" Huett, age 24, was the youngest of the Boys and was said to be the slowest of group. Jackie was 5'9," 165 pounds with brown hair and green eyes. Jackie lived on a farm with his family and loved playing with his beagle, "Beau." He also loved riding his 90 cc Honda motorcycle around his parent's property.

It was said that Jackie Huett was a loving shadow to Ted Weiher, whom he had known for eight years. Jackie looked up to Ted Weiher as if Ted were his big brother. Ted enjoyed having the younger Jackie as his sidekick and protégé. Ted would often make phone calls for Jackie because making phone calls caused Jackie to become anxious. Jackie's father said that Jackie could not read or write. He was very shy and had a speech impediment. (*Marysville Appeal Democrat*, March 2, 1978)

Jackie lived with his parents and worked doing "odds and ends" at the Gateway Projects facility in Yuba City. It was reported that Jackie had an IQ of around 40. His mother Sara was quoted as saying "He was a delight," "He was just slow, but real happy." (*Marysville Appeal Democrat*, March 2, 1978)

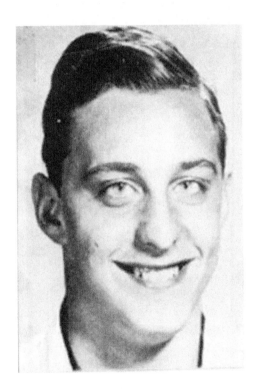

GARY MATHIAS

Previously unpublished photo of Gary Mathias,
taken a week before his disappearance.

Gary Mathias, age 25, was the newest member of the group. Gary had met the other Boys after he had become involved with the Gateway Projects and played on the Gateway Gators basketball team. Gary was 5'10" and 170 pounds with brown hair and hazel eyes. He wore thick glasses, which were prescribed for his poor eyesight. His family suggested that without them, he would be very close to seeing double. Gary's poor eyesight was the result of his falling out of a moving car after he had opened the door. This mishap was very serious, and Gary was completely blind for 4 days afterward and wound up spending several days in the hospital.

Gary, unlike the other four Boys, did not have an intellectual disability but was diagnosed with paranoid schizophrenia, which made him prone to violent outbursts. According to Tammie, Gary showed no signs of mental illness as a child. It is theorized that the serious head injury he received when he fell out of the car may have led to his mental issues.

Gary served in the U.S. Army in 1973. He was stationed in Germany and given an honorable discharge due to his mental condition. A few years after he left the Army, Gary was taking three antipsychotic medications a day to enable him to cope with his mental condition. Gary was considered by his doctors to be a success story. His treatment appeared to have kept any flare-ups in check for almost two years prior to his disappearance.

Although he lived at home with his mother and stepfather, he did have a level of independence that the other Boys did not have. Gary was able to hold down a steady job, working for his stepfather's landscaping business, where he made money to supplement his Army disability pay. Gary graduated from Marysville High School in 1971, where he had been a linebacker for the football team.

Gary was a big fan of the Rolling Stones and some time prior to his disappearance was the lead singer in a local rock band called The Fifth Shade. According to Gary's sister, the band won the first year of the Battle of the Bands at the Yuba-Sutter Fairgrounds. At the time of his disappearance, Gary was dating his high school girlfriend, Lisa.

DREW HURST BEESON

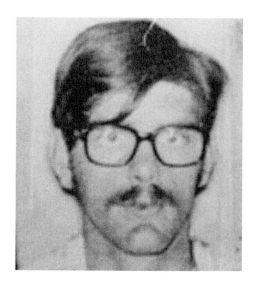

CHAPTER 2: GAME TIME

Ted Weiher had just gobbled down his dinner and was eagerly waiting to be picked up by his friends to attend the game at Chico State. Ted did not have to wait long as just moments after finishing his food, he saw Jack Madruga's prized Montego pull up in his driveway and heard Jack honk the horn. Ted briskly left the house, telling his mother that he would not need his jacket that night.

Sitting next to Jack Madruga, in the front passenger seat, was Jackie Huett. Ted climbed into the back seat of the two-door car and sat down beside Bill Sterling. The Boys then headed over to Gary Mathias' house, which was just down the street from Ted's.

Like Ted, Gary Mathias had finished his dinner just after 5:30 p.m. on Friday night and was waiting to be picked by his friends to attend the basketball game at Chico State. Despite the weather forecast of light snow that evening, Gary assured his mother and step-father that he would not need to take his jacket to the game since he was planning to come straight home after the game ended.

Like all the other Boys, Gary had laid out his basketball clothes including his "Gateway Gators" jersey in anticipation of the big game that was set to be played at 9:30 a.m. the following morning. In fact, Gary had repeatedly told his mother in the week leading up to the game, "We got a big game Saturday; don't let me oversleep."

The Boys' final stop before they left the Yuba City area was at the Mico Service Station, which Bill Sterling's parents managed, at 619 Colusa Avenue, so Bill could get his $15 weekly allowance. Bill's mother recalled that the Boys never mentioned going anywhere but the game in Chico.

From known accounts, the Boys made it to Chico and watched the entire game. Several witnesses recalled seeing them at the game, and a few recalled seeing Jack Madruga's car leave the parking lot immediately following the conclusion of the game, shortly after 10:00 p.m.

The most reliable account came from Bill Lee, the executive editor of *The Chico Enterprise – Record* newspaper. Lee stated that the five men sat by themselves, only a short distance from him. Lee was "pretty sure" that they stayed for the entire game. It was easy to observe the Boys among the small number of spectators at the game. Lee, however, did not make a connection between the men he saw at the basketball game and the missing men until the Chico newspaper published their photographs on Tuesday, February 28th.

After leaving the game, the Boys must have been in high spirits since their favorite team, the U.C. Davis Aggies, secured a road win over the Chico State Wildcats. Before leaving Chico, the Boys went to Behr's Market, just a few blocks from the Chico State basketball arena to get some snacks, which included one Hostess cherry pie, one Langendorf lemon pie, one Snickers bar, one Marathon bar, two Pepsi Colas and a quart and a half of milk for their ride home. The store night clerk, Mary Davis, recalled seeing the Boys come into the store very close to closing time, and she remembered feeling resentful that the Boys caused her to have to stay at the store longer than she had planned.

"I could tell they were a little different," Davis said, "but they were having a good time, bought some things, and then left." (*The Sacramento Bee*, March 19, 1978)

Meanwhile back at home, many of the parents had stayed up waiting for the Boys to return home. It would have been very out of character for the Boys not to tell their parents exactly where they were going and when they would home.

Ted Weiher's mother must have fallen asleep at some point during the night and was jolted out of her sleep at 5 a.m. Making her way to Ted's room and seeing that his bed was empty, Imogene Weiher began to panic, and although it was still early in the morning, she made a phone call to Bill Sterling's mother, Juanita, who had been awake since 2 a.m. Juanita told Imogene that Bill had not returned home either, and she must have been in a near panic herself.

Bill Sterling's mother had already called Jack Madruga's mother, who relayed that Jack had not come home either. Ted Weiher's mother called Jackie Huett's mother, and Mrs. Weiher's daughter-in-law walked to nearby Gary Mathias' house to inform his stepfather. It was then confirmed that all five Boys had vanished. At 8 p.m. that evening, Jack Madruga's mother called the police.

After Sunday passed with still no sign of the Boys, the Yuba County Sheriff's Office started an investigation with Lieutenant Lance Ayres in charge of the search for the Boys. The Sheriff's Office put out a nationwide bulletin for the missing Boys and began to search for them in earnest. Having grown up in Marysville and having attended Marysville High School with Ted Weiher and his two brothers, Dallas and Perry Weiher, Ayres had a personal connection to the Boys.

Lance J. Ayres (1945 – 2010)

Ayres expanded the search area, and Jack Madruga's turquoise Mercury Montego was found on Monday, February 27, on a rural gravel recreational mountain road in the Plumas National Forest at an elevation of 4,400 feet. The car was seen by a Forest Ranger, William Burris, who was in the woods making timber, on February 25, the day after the Boys went to the basketball game, but Burris did not consider it unusual for a car to be at that location since local residents would sometimes park on the road on weekends and go skiing. Burris reported his find after seeing a news report on the missing men in which the vehicle was mentioned.

The specific site where the car was found was in Butte County's rugged Rogers Cow Camp area northeast of the town of Oroville, California.

Rogers Cow Camp Campground

This mountain area was seventy miles away from Chico, where the Boys had attended the basketball game, and approximately seventy miles from the Yuba City area, where the Boys lived. Heavy snow had fallen in the area and had covered the car since the Boys' disappearance.

The car was found right at the snowline. Although it looked like the car had become stuck in 10 inches of snow and had spun its tires, the car did not appear to be so badly stuck that five grown men could not have easily pushed it out. It was further noted that the car had a quarter of a tank of gas, and it started easily when police hotwired it and drove it to nearby Oroville. There appeared to be no reason that the car would have stopped running, so why did the Boys abandon it?

Despite the fact that the rural road was heavily rutted, the police later noted that the bottom of the car had no signs of damage; even the muffler, which was relatively low to the ground, was not damaged, leading the police to believe that whoever had driven the car up that mountain road must have been very familiar with it, especially given the fact that the car was apparently driven up that road at night. None of the Boys were familiar with that area or that road.

According to *The Washington Post*, June 14, 1978, ". . . the car's underside was undamaged. This heavy American car, with a low-hanging muffler and presumably with five full-grown men inside, had wound up on a stretch of tortuously bumpy mountain road - apparently in total darkness - without a gouge or dent or thick mud stain to show for it. The driver had either used astonishing care and precision, the investigators figured, or else he knew the road well enough to anticipate every rut."

When the car was discovered, one of its windows was partially rolled down, and the doors were locked. The keys were not in the ignition. Food and candy wrappers from the items the Boys had purchased from Behr's market were lying on the seats. Family members said that Jack would never have left his car unsecured. Jack's mother said that the Montego was Jack's baby, and under ordinary circumstances, he never would have left the way it was found. *(The Washington Post, June 14, 1978)*

Photo of Jack Madruga's 1969 Mercury Montego, taken after it was recovered from the mountain location where it was abandoned.
Marysville Appeal Democrat, March 2, 1978.

There simply was no reasonable explanation for the Boys' deciding to drive up that cold dark mountain road that night. Some considered that they just took a wrong turn and wound up lost on the desolate highway, but if they were lost, why had they not opened one of the four perfectly folded maps, including one of California, that were in the glove compartment of Jack's Montego? Why would they abandon a mechanically sound car? Nothing added up.

According to family members, none of the men knew that area at all. Bill Sterling's father, Jim, told the police that some eight years earlier, he had taken Bill fishing in an area not very far from where the car was found, but Bill had hated the experience and did not go back with his family on the few subsequent trips they made there. The Madrugas asserted that Jack did not like camping or being out in the cold, especially without a heavy coat. Ted Weiher's family relayed that although years earlier, Ted had been on a hunting trip in a location that was not far from where the car was found, he did not like the outdoors. *(Marysville Appeal Democrat*, Marysville, CA, March 2,

1978)

1969 Mercury Montego,
similar to the car that Jack Madruga owned

The discovery of Jack Madruga's car was the beginning of a mystery that to this day remains unsolved.

Hope fades for 5

MARYSVILLE, Calif. (AP) — Despite scores of tips, a $4,000 reward, some footprints in the snow and scraps of cloth tied around trees, officials still have no idea what hap-
pened to five slightly retarded

CHAPTER 3: ONE HUNDRED DAYS

The Search

Forest rangers searched the area where the car was discovered and found no trace of the Boys. Soon after the search had started, a severe blizzard moved into the mountain area, covering any tracks the Boys may have left. Around nine inches of snow dropped on the upper mountain.

On March 2, about fifty men, some on snowcats (fully tracked trucks designed to move on snow) took part in the search. Jack Huett, Sr., along with his dog, Beau, searched on snowmobile for his son. He believed that Jackie and the other Boys could generally take care of themselves, but he also knew that they were very trusting and impressionable. As the snowdrifts became higher, some of the searchers themselves almost became lost.

Jack Huett, Sr.

On March 7, searchers on horseback and four wheelers began to explore the structures in the foothill area north of Marysville-Dobbins Road. Jack Beecham organized an eight-man task force to coordinate the searches, with Plumas, Yuba, and Butte counties pooling resources.

Beecham is quoted as saying, "We have no evidence of foul play, but we are looking at the possibility because this is so out of character for the missing men." (*Marysville Appeal Democrat,* March 2, 1978)

The Witness on the Oroville-Quincy Highway

Although the exact date is not known, a man named Joseph Schons (often misspelled as Shones), age 55, of Berry Creek came forward after hearing about the missing men. Schons told the police that he had inadvertently wound up spending the night of February 24 -25 near the area where Jack Madruga's Montego was found.

He had driven up the road to check the snowpack in preparation for a weekend ski trip he was planning to spend with his wife and daughter at a cabin he owned in the area. Sometime around 5:30 p.m. that Friday afternoon, about 150 feet up the road, he got his Volkswagen Beetle stuck in the snow. While attempting to free his car from the snow, Schons realized that he was beginning to experience the early symptoms of a heart attack and got back into his car, keeping the engine running to provide heat.

Some six hours later, around 11:30 p.m., still sitting in his car experiencing terrible pain, Schons said that he heard "whistling sounds" and then noticed a car parked about 20 feet behind him. Schons got out of his car and saw five or six people around that other car, backlit by their headlights, sometime between 11 p.m. and midnight on the 24th, the night of the basketball game. Schons could not get a clear look at the people; they appeared shadowy in the darkness, illuminated only by their car's lights.

He did say that he thought that one of the people may have been a woman, holding what looked like a baby in her arms. Schons called out to the group of people for help, but the shadowy figures did not acknowledge him and suddenly went back towards their car. Then the headlights went out, and the talking stopped. A sudden eerie silence came over the area again.

Schons then got back into his car to stay warm. About two hours later, Schons again heard whistling noises and got out of his car again. Regaining his strength, he made his way towards a car that was parked on the road, down the hill from his car, and saw what looked like flashlight beams. As he got closer to the car, he could see that it was the same car that he had seen earlier, still parked behind him. He again called out for help, and again all the lights went out.

"I was very angry [that the people refused to help me]," Schons later said. (*The Los Angeles Times*, March 10, 1978)

At about 4:00 a.m., Schons' car ran out of gas, and the heater went off. He then started walking towards the car that he had seen earlier in the night, about fifty yards away. When he reached the car, which he later confirmed was Jack's Mercury, no one was around. He then shouted and "nothing stirred." Next, he looked through the partially-rolled-down window and saw nothing unusual inside. Schons could not recall if the keys were in the ignition.

He then made a five mile walk back down the road toward a restaurant called the Mountain House Lodge, where he had stopped earlier in the night to get a drink on his way up the mountain. After reaching the lodge, he said he was given a ride to the Oroville Hospital.

It was later confirmed that indeed Schons had suffered a heart attack. There are differing versions of the account from Joe Schons. I do not know if these discrepancies exist because Schons had frequently altered his story, or if these discrepancies were caused by errors in the newspaper reports or both.

One account says that he got a ride at the lodge back home; then his wife took him to the hospital. According to an account he gave to the *Los Angeles Times*, Mar 10, 1978, Schons said that he saw a "pickup" truck behind the car but does not remember why he said that. He added "I was half-conscious, not lucid, hallucinating and in deep pain. Whether I half-saw or half-imagined the second vehicle, I just don't know."

Upon learning of Schons' story, Ted Weiher's mother, Imogene Weiher, noted that her son would have responded if Schons had called for help. "Ted and Bill Sterling once helped a person get to the hospital who had overdosed on Valium," she said. (*Los Angeles Times*, March 10, 1978)

A Sightings of the Boys

A woman in the town of Brownsville in Yuba County, who asked to remain anonymous, reported to police that she recalled seeing five men in a red 1960s model pickup truck parked in front of Mary's County Store in Brownsville. Brownsville is about an hour's drive from the spot where Jack Madruga's car was found. She noted seeing a total of five men: two men in the pickup, two men using a phone booth, and a fifth man in the store. She said a man who matched Huett's description was on the telephone for 15 minutes. Huett's mother, Sarah Huett later said her son would have never spent that much time on a phone as he was unable to dial or speak at length on the phone because his mind could not relate to reaching a person over a wire. (*The Sacramento Bee*, March 19, 1978)

The woman did not report her sighting until she saw a reward poster with photos of the missing men on it.

*Pickup truck similar to the one seen by the witness at
Mary's Country Store in Brownsville*

The woman was quoted in the *Los Angeles Times* article as stating, "I noticed them because they didn't look like they came from this [Brownsville] area. And you notice strangers around here, especially them with their big eyes and facial expressions."

Lt. Dennis Moore of the Yuba County Sheriff's Office said that he believes "she is a credible witness, and we take her information seriously." (*Los Angeles Times*, March 10, 1978)

Carroll Waltz, the owner of the store, also said he saw several of the men on both Saturday, February 25, the day after the basketball game, and Sunday, February 26. Mr. Waltz was quoted in *The LA Times* as saying, "I'm pretty sure I saw [Weiher and Huett] buying burritos, chocolate milk and soft drinks." Waltz added, "I can't be positive, but I remember after she [the woman witness] asked me if I had seen the poster."

Ted Weiher's brother Dallas remarked that his brother liked to "eat everything he could get his hand on," and that Jackie Huett was Ted's "inseparable companion." "So, the store thing sounds pretty logical, but everything else about the [Brownsville] story is completely out of character." he said. (*The Sacramento Bee*, March

19, 1978)

On March 8, the Sheriff's Office investigated a cabin in the woods near Forbestown after a forest ranger had seen a red pickup truck matching the description of the one seen by Waltz and Schons parked near it. When law enforcement arrived at the cabin, the truck was no longer there, and the cabin appeared not to have been recently occupied. Searchers, with helicopter assistance, also combed Slate Creek Canyon, Strawberry Valley, and Devil's Ridge.

March 9 was the last day of the initial search as subsequent searches were reluctantly postponed until spring because the area had become heavily blanketed in snow. A headline in the *Marysville Appeal Democrat* newspaper on March 21, 1978, read "Butte Calls off Hunt for Five." The article stated that a helicopter search of the Soap Stone Canyon area near the Mountain House Lodge "failed to turn up any trace of the five missing Yuba-Sutter men."

Butte Calls Off Hunt For Five

A helicopter search of the Soap Stone Canyon area near Mountain House yesterday failed to turn up any trace of the five missing Yuba-Sutter men, and Butte County authorities have called off the search there.

"Right now, we're out of leads, Lt. Ken Mickelson said.

The five mildly retarded men have been missing since Feb. 24, when they left their homes here to attend a basketball game in Chico. They were seen at the game and at a market near the Cal State Chico campus after the game, and their car was found abandoned on a

them could identify it.

The strip of cotton cloth could have been cut from a shirt. Ayers said. It was weathered but did not appear to have been exposed to the weather for an extremely long period of time, he said.

Ayers said information continues to come into the sheriff's office on the case and each new lead is being followed up.

The missing men are:

Jack Madruga, 30, and Jack Huett, 24, both of Linda; William Sterling, 29, of Yuba City; and Ted Weiher, 30, and Gary Mathias, 25, both of Olivehurst.

Sheriff Beecham told a newspaper reporter, "It's very heavily forested country, rough and mountainous and rocky. Some places you can only get in on horseback." Beecham also noted that a study of the personalities of the missing men showed their disappearance to be totally out of character. "In fact, as time goes on, it looks more and more like foul play." (*Middletown Journal*, Middletown, Ohio. March 9, 1978, page 1)

Although the area could not be effectively searched, law enforcement and the families of the Boys did everything possible to find them. A reward of $2,600 dollars was raised by the families, and they stayed close to their telephones, desperate for any news of the whereabouts of the Boys.

Imogene Weiher

"They just disappeared from the face of the earth."
Melba Madruga, Jack Madruga's mother

At the suggestion of Melba Madruga, the families of the Boys brought in a Yuba area psychic, Dr. Gloria Elizabeth Daniel of the Marysville branch of the Church of Tzaddi, to see if she could help to locate the Boys. After the meeting, Dr. Daniel made a tape recording of her psychic visions, which included certain areas and some numbers that she perceived could be a house address where the Boys were being held.

Yuba County Undersheriff Jack Beecham said that he reviewed the tape, but the search areas mentioned by Dr. Daniel were areas that had been searched already. Lt. Ayers is on record as saying that he did search for the house that the psychic saw, but to no avail.

The reported sightings of the Boys gave their families hope, but each sighting failed to bring the Boys back home. The families were tearing their hearts out, racking their brains, and bouncing theories off each other. One of their theories centered around a friend of Gary Mathias, a friend who lived in Forbestown, California. Could Gary's friend know something about what had happened to the Boys? Could that friend have been involved?

Despite its name, Forbestown was (and still is) hardly a town. A former mining center, by 1978 Forbestown was more of a ghost town, dotted with woodlands, cabins, and delapidated mining equipment, and inhabited by people who seemed to enjoy Forbestown's remoteness more for the opportunity it provided to engage in criminal activity than for the chance it gave them to commune with nature.

Forbestown Post Office
date of photo unknown

Could Gary have wanted to see his friend in Forbestown and persuaded the Boys to stop there on their way home from the basketball game? If the Boys had planned to leave Chico and go to Forbestown, they could easily have missed a turn and become lost, ending up on Oroville-Quincy Highway. Could the Boys have ended up in Forbestown?

Bob Klopf, Gary Mathias' stepfather, did not think so. According to Klopf, Mathias liked his Forbestown friend well enough to stop by his home if he were in the area, but he would not have stopped to visit him the night before a big game.

"I don't believe the five were ever in the area. I think they're either in the lake or six feet under brush somewhere," Klopf concluded. "You have to think about that now." (*Middletown Journal*, March 9, 1978)

But Imogene Weiher and Cathy Madruga, Jack Madruga's 23-year-old niece, were not ready to think about that yet. Imogene and Cathy were thinking that the Boys were possibly being held against their will in Forbestown.

And Cathy was going to go there and find them, with the assistance of her best friend Ann and her brother George.

"George, come on, we can't waste another second!" Cathy called out as she walked through George's front door to get to her car waiting in the driveway. "If the Boys are up there, they need us to get there as soon as possible, and I told Grandma Melba to call the sheriff if we're not back in two hours, so we need to get a move on!"

George immediately followed her through the door, and Cathy handed him her keys. "Would you please drive and wait for us in the car – in case we need to make a quick getaway?"

George nodded, stuck out his right hand, palm-side up, and Cathy plunked down her keys into it.

Cathy then turned to her best friend, who was walking beside her, and said, "Ann, thank you so much for going with me. You are a true friend."

"Cathy," Ann responded. "I would do anything to help. I love Doc, too."

The three piled into Cathy's '75 Dodge Dart, each one saying a silent prayer, and George backed out of the driveway onto the street, and they were on their way to Forbestown.

Forbestown is just a few miles north of Brownsville, but it seemed to take forever to get there. Ann fidgeted in the back seat, and Cathy mostly just looked out the passenger-side window, noticing the trees and the different sizes of the rocks on the shoulders and the gas stations and the houses and the cars in people's driveways as they passed them by. She wondered if the people in the houses were happy to be alive, and she wondered if the people in the houses knew what it felt like to wonder if someone you love is alive. And she prayed.

Cathy noticed that the trees were becoming taller and the brush was getting thicker as they got farther away from civilization. They were getting closer to their destination, so Cathy figured that another prayer was in order. She was just in the middle of that prayer when they drove past Forbestown's tiny post office/general store.

From the post office, it took only a minute or two to get to Mathias' friend's house. They knew they were getting close when they drove into a tripwire stretched across the road and saw men with rifles and shotguns, trying to hide in the woods.

"Drug dealers," Cathy thought to herself.

She had heard about some of the shady things that went on up here in the woods, and she knew that there were booby traps all over, bear traps waiting for an unsuspecting curious person to walk into. Gary's friend and Gary's friend's friends did want outsiders coming onto their property, and they were armed and ruthless. But Cathy was more angry than afraid as they came upon a house trailer with 3 or 4 sheds behind it. One shed was boarded up.

Cathy got out of the car, dragging Ann behind her, and carefully stepping over bottles, cans, and assorted debris, she walked to the trailer's front door and knocked. Cathy and Ann could hear a baby crying inside, but nobody answered the door. Cathy knocked again. Still no answer.

As they stood at the front door, the women noticed a small girl moving in the trees behind the trailer. They also noticed a baby stroller and some cut wood stacked near one of the sheds. There was something about that shed. Something strange. It was a shabby-looking wooden shed with a metal roof and weeds almost as tall as a man growing all around it. It had a metal bar instead of a door handle, with a sort of concealed screw surface bolt with a hole in it that the notch in the metal bar fit over. The bolt was turned to keep the door closed, and a padlock had been placed through the hole in the bolt to keep the door locked. She wondered what was in that shed. What was so valuable in that shed that it was kept locked up here in the middle of nowhere? She thought for a moment and then she knew – Gary Mathias was in that shed.

She ran to the shed and pounded on the door crying, "Gary! Gary!" But there was no answer.

She pulled on the padlock that kept the door shut tight. She kicked the door, switching from her right foot to her left when her foot started hurting.

She listened for sounds coming from inside. Nothing. She heard nothing, but Cathy knew that Gary was in that shed. She felt it.

She decided to try to find something to pry the door open or to smash it down. "With all this junk around here, there has to be something I can use," she said to herself as she walked toward a shed that appeared to be unlocked.

"There might be tools in there," she thought.

Ann had stayed near the front door of the trailer, looking for signs of trouble, mainly in the form of men with guns coming toward them, but she ran to join Cathy as soon as she had heard her call Gary's name. They had just opened the unlocked shed's door when they heard a car horn and heard George yell, "Cathy, Ann get in the car!"

The women raced to the car and saw George, sitting in the driver's seat, talking to a weathered-looking man standing beside the car, his left hand on the driver's side mirror and his right hand wrapped around a Remington 870.

George looked at Cathy and Ann. "This gentleman has asked us to leave. I think we had better do so," he explained.

Ann dutifully and sensibly got into the back seat, but Cathy was not quite ready to go.

"Do you know Gary Mathias?" she asked the man, looking directly into his eyes.

The man locked eyes with her and simply said, "No." Then he added, "Get off my property."

But Cathy was not done with him. "Gary Mathias is in that shed, and I am not leaving until I get him out," she said with more authority than she had ever spoken with before.

It was not enough authority, however, and the man replied by pumping his shotgun. With that action, he had made a compelling argument for the trespassers to leave, and Cathy quickly got into the car, and the three of them drove to the safety of home.

Once home, Cathy called the Sheriff's Office, told them what had occurred, hung up, and waited for them to tell her what they found after they investigated the trailer in Forbestown. The wait was not long, what they found was not much, and what they said was rather suspicious – so suspicious that Cathy knew that they had not gone up to Forbestown at all. The Sheriff's Office told her that they had checked out the property on horseback, but Cathy knew that was not possible because the area surrounding the trailer home was pocketed with booby traps. A horse walking there would surely have become ensnared in a bear trap.

"So much for law enforcement," Cathy said to herself. "Sometimes when you want justice, you have to carry it out yourself."

Law Enforcement claimed that officers did contact people in Forbestown who knew Gary. These "friends" told the officers that they had not seen Gary in over a year.

No credible sightings of the Boys, other than the Schons and Brownsville accounts, were reported to police. Law enforcement searched over thirty stores along the route that the Boys must have taken from the basketball game in Chico to Oroville, but they turned up nothing. Search volunteers in Butte County spent 4,000 man-hours looking in the foothill area. Search base camps were set-up and manned for six days as dozens of men combed the hills and gullies each day in a 42 square-mile area along 250 miles of mountain roadway. A Highway Patrol Helicopter flew over the region and still turned up nothing. All searchers who participated in looking for the Yuba Boys were baffled that their efforts did not produce any results.

No trace of 5 missing handicapped men

MARYSVILLE (UPI) — There is still no trace of five mentally handicapped men who have been missing for more than two weeks after attending a basketball game 50 miles away in Chico.

"We've searched every place possible," said Yuba County Sheriff Jim Grant Sunday. "There's not a trace of these men. We don't even have any evidence of foul play."

The men, all from the Marysville area, are identified as Jack Madruga, 30, Jack Huett, 24, Ted Weiher, 30, Gary Mathias, 25, and William Sterling, 29.

All five had mental handicaps, Grant said, but none of the five required hospitalization and all lived with their families in the area.

The case was very frustrating for authorities, and Lance Ayers stated that he was "tearing his hair out. The more time elapses, the less chance there is of finding them alive." (*State Times Advocate*, March 28, 1978)

While the families tried to remain hopeful, they knew that some disreputable people lived in the mountains, and they were concerned that their sons had met with foul play. A good description of the type of people that the Boys may have encountered along the Oroville-Quincy Highway comes from an anonymous person on a Yuba County Five internet message board. The writer describes a frightening incident that took place in the area where Jack Madruga's car was abandoned.

Posted under a pseudonym:

> I used to live less than a mile from where the Mercury Montego was found. I now live in Oroville, and I am not surprised by this mystery. There are some very scary characters living up in the Berry Creek, Mountain House, and French Creek Areas. I was confronted by two very disturbing men way back in the woods while camping up at a site called "Haphazard," which is down a long gravel road where the "Rogers Cow Camp" campsite is located in French Creek. This location is just off highway 162 and less than 50 yards from where the Mercury Montego was found.
>
> Fortunately, I am a Combat Veteran and had a very strange feeling in my gut that something was off as soon as I arrived at the campsite early that morning. Additionally, I was very well armed as I always am when in a remote wooded area due to common sense and a life-threatening experience I had as a teen with a large hungry mountain lion.
>
> So, these two "Deliverance" looking mountain men started approaching me from two separate directions, making it obvious that I had been watched for some

time. The crunch of fallen dry pine needles and the snapping of small brush from the left and right was immediately followed by me cocking my Colt Python 357 Magnum as I pulled it from my waistband and asked in a loud stern voice "You motherf**kers must be tired of breathing coming at me like this out here."

They claimed they didn't see me and apologized then headed east through the woods looking back at me a couple times to see if I was still watching. I returned to camp just as my girlfriend and a few of my buddies and their wives were pulling in. I told them what had happened in the woods. The weirdos obviously had been sneaking around watching us that first night because a couple times we heard screaming from the surrounding woods when they stepped on the 4" inch wood screws we had sticking up through the pallet boards originally brought for kindling but later used as "Warning Devices" we placed out in the woods surrounding our campsite while we acted like we were gathering firewood.

The second night was scream free, but we watched with my infrared night scope a group of three men sneaking around out in the woods as if they were on some type of mission. They finally headed back where they came from around 2:30 a.m. Good thing they did too, because we were very tired of their sh*t and quite irritated and just wanted to go to bed. So, no telling what could have happened if they insisted on harassing us.

CHAPTER 4: FOUR ARE FOUND

One hundred agonizing days had gone by since the Boys from Yuba County had gone missing - one hundred days without any answers.

On Sunday, June 4, 1978, that suddenly changed when a small group of recreational motorcycle riders happened upon an abandoned U.S. Forest Service trailer camp in a cul-de-sac just beyond a grove of trees. It was not unusual for a Forest Service Station in a remote area to be unmanned since some of these stations were only used when needed for wildfire spotting or an occasional search and rescue mission.

It was a sunny day and starting to get warm as the sun beat down on the beautiful mountain landscape. The motorcyclists had been riding for the better part of the day and decided to take a break by pulling off the main road into a deserted camp in the Daniel Zink Campgrounds. The camp consisted of one large main trailer surrounded by four smaller trailers. One of the motorcycle riders removed his helmet and was immediately overcome by a nauseating, putrid smell that seemed to be coming from the main trailer.

Thinking that this smell must be coming from a dead animal, the man glanced around, looking for a carcass, and noticed a broken window on the main trailer. Not seeing a dead animal on the ground, he thought that perhaps an animal had gotten into the trailer and had died, so he decided to see what was inside. What the man saw through the window would be not only the beginning of finding some answers to this case, but also the beginning of an avalanche of new questions that still go unanswered over forty years later.

A JUSTICE STORY

Mystery of the Sierra Nevada

The Daily News, New York, NY, Jan. 7, 1979.
*Depiction of the motorcycle riders pulling up to the forest
service trailer where Ted Weiher's body was found*

What the man saw through the window was the emaciated body of Ted Weiher, lying face up, stretched out on a bunk bed with his hand on his chest. The motorcyclist described what he saw, "Both of his pant legs were rolled up above his knees, revealing apparent blood poisoning and gangrene." (*Sacramento Bee*, February 26, 2019)

It appeared that the man had frozen to death. The motorcycle riders left the camp and reported what they had found.

Several bed sheets had been pulled over Ted Wehier's body up to his chin. His leather shoes were off his feet and missing. Five of Ted's toes were missing due to acute frostbite, and his feet were severely frostbitten, giving way to gangrene. Given the condition of Ted's feet, he could not have pulled the bed sheets over himself because it would have been too painful, so law enforcement concluded that there must have been at least one other person with him in the trailer. There was no indication of foul play according to Plumas County Assistant Sheriff Dave Wingfield.

On a table by the bed was Ted's ring with "Ted" engraved on it, his gold necklace, his wallet (with cash inside), and a gold Waltham watch with its crystal missing. The families all stated that the watch did not belong to any of the five men.

A Waltham watch similar to the one found on a table near Ted Weiher's body.

A single partially melted candle was also on the table, the only known source of light and heat in the trailer. There were several paperback books and pieces of furniture in the trailer that could have been (but were not) used to build a fire for warmth to fight the bitter mountain cold. Matches that Ted could have used to start a fire were also found in the trailer. In a shed outside, there was a full propane tank that if only switched on would have provided the trailer with heat. When searchers found the tank, they noticed that the door to the shed was partially blocked by snow. It is possible that when the Boys found the trailer, there may have been even more snow in front of the shed.

Also at Ted's disposal in the trailer were extra blankets, extra clothing, and plenty of food. As explained by Deputy Sheriff Dennis Forcino of the Plumas County Sheriff's Department in the June 13, *Napa Valley Register*, either he [Weiher] or another of the victims "busted into a shed outside and got C rations. Three cases were completely consumed. Each case contains twelve individual meals, things like stew, can of crackers, can of fruit. A total of 36 meals were eaten."

Next to where the C rations were stored, was an unlocked cabinet with enough dehydrated meals "to last an Army," said another Deputy. (*Napa Valley Register*, June 13, 1978)

Ted was 5'11" and 200 pounds at the time he went missing, but when he was found, he had lost from 80 to 100 pounds. It has been determined by a Plumas County pathologist that based on the growth of the beard on his face, Ted had lived in "starving agony" in the trailer from eight to thirteen weeks before he succumbed to exposure, just two weeks before his body was found. (*New York Daily News* January 7, 1979)

Ted Weiher, 1963

Upon autopsy, it was discovered that Weiher had died of pulmonary congestion due to exposure, and not of starvation or hypothermia as has been frequently reported. Pulmonary congestion, often called wet lung, is caused by exposure to the cold and is similar to pneumonia.

We can only speculate about why there appeared to be no attempt to build a fire to keep warm. It is is also unknown why Ted became emaciated in the midst of enough canned food to last for months.

According to reports, at least some of the meals had been opened with an Army P-38 can opener, a small sickle-shaped device.

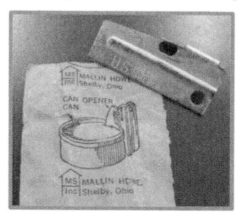

U.S. Army P-38 can opener

The only two men who knew how to use this type of can opener were Jack Madruga and Gary Mathias as both had served in the Army. This is evidence that Gary Mathias and/or Jack Madruga were in the trailer for some time with Ted Weiher, which leads to another question: if Gary were at the trailer, why didn't he build a fire? He would have been completely capable of doing so. Could the men have been afraid to build a fire for fear that it would call attention to where they were? What could have frightened the men that much?

As Bob Klopf, Gary's stepfather, put it, "I can't understand why Gary would have been that scared. All those paperbacks, and they didn't even build a lousy fire. I can't understand why they didn't do that unless they were afraid." (Gorney, 5 'Boys' Who Never Come Back, *The Washington Post*, July 6, 1978)

DEATH SCENE—A searcher walks up to the Forest Service bunkhouse where Ted Weiher, 32, died from exposure. The camp is about seven miles from where five Yuba-Sutter men abandoned their car in a snowbank. Weiher is believed to have lived several weeks in the bunkhouse before succumbing. Authorities in Plumas and Butte counties say they were not aware the bunkhouse was kept there during the winter and for some reason the Forest Service did not tell them. The body of Jack Huett, 24, of Linda, was found yesterday about a quarter of a mile from the bunkhouse, and the bodies of William Sterling, 29, of Yuba City, and Jack Madruga, 30, of Linda about three and one-half miles from it. Photo by Dennis R. Warren.

As some of the tragic pieces of the puzzle were starting to come into place, the nightmare of discovering the full depth of the Boys' suffering during their fight for survival was only just beginning.

The recovery of Ted Weiher's body led to intense emotions for all of the Boys' families. Over the course of several conversations with Jack Madruga's niece Cathy (who was 23 years old at the time of her uncle's disappearance), I have gained real insight into the emotional turmoil experienced by the families of the Yuba County Five. In times of crisis, it is natural for family members to cling to each other for support, and it was this emotional support that two members of the Madruga family provided each other when Cathy moved in with her grandmother, Jack's mother, "Grandma Melba," shortly after the Boys' disappearance.

61

The spring of 1978 was, of course, a time of worrying and wondering for Cathy and Grandma Melba, but it was also a time of hoping and praying: hoping for information, hoping for resolution, praying that Doc was safe somewhere – safe and alive. The Madruga family would cling to that hope, even as it got fainter with each passing day, until June 6, 1978 when they received word that Doc's body had been found – all of the Madruga family, that is, except for Cathy, whose hopes were destroyed the night before the discovery.

The evening of June 5, 1978 was not much different from any of the other evenings that had passed since Doc had gone missing. Cathy was just going through the motions of life, trying to find comfort in routine mindless tasks, trying to ease the pain of her overwhelming grief through work. But the only real escape she had was sleep, and it was sleep that she looked forward to as she settled down for the night in Doc's bedroom, where she had been sleeping since she had come to stay with Grandma Melba.

Cathy loved Doc's bedroom. His Gateway Gators jersey was hanging on the hook on his bedroom door, carefully placed on a hangar in anticipation of the big game, and his basketball shoes were in the corner, waiting for him to come home. Although they never said so out loud, Grandma Melba and Cathy dared not put away Doc's basketball things – moving them would be an admission that Jack was never coming home. And with his things still laid out, laid out by his own hand, it was almost as if he were home. And when he did come home . . . When he did come home, Grandma Melba would make him his favorite chocolate cake, the whole family would be at the house, and Cathy would hug her uncle and never let him go.

It was while thinking of these things that Cathy fell asleep. The first thing Cathy noticed as her mind slipped into dreamy darkness was the sound of someone's sobbing. As she continued to listen, the sobs became louder, and she realized that she was hearing a man crying. And it was not just any man – it sounded like Doc! She strained to see him, but all she could see was inky blackness.

"Doc! Doc! Is that you? Doc! Please don't cry!" she called out. And then she saw him coming out of the darkness, still crying. She tried to get to him, but as she reached toward him, Doc slipped back into the shadows, and Cathy slipped back into wakefulness, wondering if what she had experienced was dream or reality. One thing she now knew for sure – Doc was not coming home. Doc was gone.

The enormity of this realization shook her to the core and made it difficult for her to get out of bed and face another day. Another day without Doc. All the rest of her days without Doc. She lay in bed, immobile, too shaken to move, too shaken to cry, exhausted by emotion. What if she never moved? What if she never got up? What if . . . Her thoughts were interrupted by Grandma Melba's rustling around in the kitchen.

"Cathy, you up? Want some coffee?" Grandma Melba shouted through the door.

"Ummmmm," Cathy responded, stirring in bed, still not wanting to get up. Then a thought struck her. *What if Grandma Melba needs me?* And with that thought, she planted her feet on the floor and into the slippers that she kept beside the bed. *I have to be strong for Grandma Melba.*

"Be right there, Grandma," she said, and went out of Doc's bedroom and into the bathroom down the hall.

A few minutes later, Cathy walked into the kitchen as Grandma Melba was pouring herself a cup of coffee.

"Good morning, Grandma," Cathy said as she grabbed a mug from the wooden coffee-cup tree on the counter.

"Good morning, dear," her grandmother replied. "How did you sleep?"

"Well," Cathy hesitated. "Well, I had a disturbing dream and . . ."

A knock at the door interrupted Cathy's story. She looked at Grandma Melba. "That's the police. They're here to tell us that they found Doc's body," she said, trying to keep her emotions in check as she went to the door.

It *was* the police, and they had grim news. Cathy and Grandma Melba hugged each other and burst into tears.

Jack "Doc" Madruga, Vietnam ca.1968

Jack Madruga's body was the second of the Yuba County Five's to be recovered. After Ted Weiher's body had been found on Sunday, June 4, a massive search had been launched in the area around the Forest Service camp. On Tuesday, June 6, a local man named Tom Dean, who was using his tracking dogs to help with the search, was driving down the service road with his dogs in the back of his truck when one of the dogs alerted Tom to a field just off the main road. This was how Jack Madruga's body was discovered.

Sheriff Forcino was the person to find Bill Sterling's body, 15 feet off the road. Jim Sterling was the second person on the scene. Sterling's father asked the sheriff how he knew he that it was his son's body that he had found, and the Sheriff replied, "Sir, we found the wallet. It has pictures [of Bill's twin sisters] and his social security card." (*The Napa Valley Register*, Napa, California, June 13, 1978)

With his worst fears now confirmed, Jim Sterling broke down and began sobbing as he fell to his knees.

The Sacramento Bee, June 7, 1978
The caption reads "Jim Sterling, right, is comforted by a friend near the site where the body of his son William was found.

The bodies of Jack Madruga and Bill Sterling were found four and half miles away from the trailer where Ted Weiher's body had been found, on opposite sides of the mountain road that led to the trailer, about eleven miles from their abandoned car. Jack Madruga's body was found near a stream. The bodies of both Sterling and Madruga were both badly ravaged by wild animals. Bill Sterling's skull was found 50 yards away from the rest of his body. Madruga's right arm had been bitten off. He was found lying on his side, clutching his watch in his left hand. Madruga's car keys were in his pants pocket. Sheriff Forcino speculated that Madruga was tired and collapsed on the side of the road, and Sterling refused to leave his side.

The next day, June 7, Jackie Huett's body was found two and a half miles from the trailer by his brother-in-law's brother, who was taking part in the search. Wild animals had scattered Jackie's remains. His skull was found 100 yards from the rest of his body. In the July 6, 1978 article in *The Washington Post* titled "5 'Boys' Who Never Came Back," it was reported that Jackie Huett's father found his son's backbone as it fell out of Jackie's clothing. It was further stated that Lt. Ayres had tried to talk the elder Huett out of taking part in the search, fearing something like that may happen, but Huett had insisted.

The identities of Huett, Madruga, and Sterling were confirmed by dental records.

"As cold as it must have been, they probably just got tired and wanted to lay down and go to sleep If you let yourself do that, well . . . ," stated Deputy Dennis Forcino. (*Napa Valley Register*, June

13, 1978)

Part of the mystery was finally over. Despite continued searches of the area, the body of Gary Mathias was never found, and he is listed as missing to this day. Gary's stepfather, Robert Klopf, was sure that searchers would eventually find Gary's thick-rimmed glasses as "an animal would not eat them." (Gorney, 5 'Boys' Who Never Come Back, *The Washington Post*, July 6, 1978)

Gary's family was as distraught as the other families since they still had no answers about what may have happened to Gary.

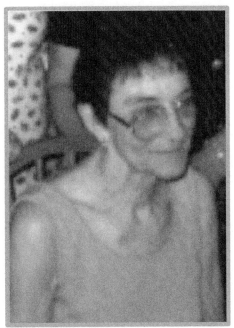

Ida Klopf, Gary Mathias' mother
Ida Klopf said she didn't turn on the TV for weeks because she didn't want to find out the bad news that way. She said that she was going up to look for her son herself.

Investigators now had their work cut out for them: trying to figure out how the Yuba County Five made it so far up the mountain on foot, wearing street clothes with no jackets, in freezing temperatures and 3 - 6 foot snowdrifts. An even bigger question was why the Boys had left their perfectly running car in the first place.

The day before the Boys went missing, a Forest Service snowcat was driven to the trailer camp, so a Forest Service worker could get the snow off the main trailer roof, so it would not collapse. It was speculated that the Boys found the packed path made by the Snowcat and believed that it would take them to shelter not far away. It was further believed by investigators that Jack Madruga and Bill Sterling succumbed to hypothermia halfway to the trailer.

A snowcat

CHAPTER 5: THE INVESTIGATION CONTINUES

Most newspaper reports stated that the distance from where Jack's car was abandoned to where the trailer was located was approximately 19 miles. Using the information in the very detailed June 13, 1978 *Napa Valley Register* article that stated that the U.S. Forest Service Camp trailer was located in the Daniel Zink Campground area, and the March 10, 1978 *Los Angeles Times* article that stated that Jack Madruga's car was abandoned in "Butte County's rugged Rogers Cow Camp area," I was able to map out the distance by road from the spot where the car was left (Rogers Cow Camp Campground, which is slightly northwest of the former community of Merrimac along the Oroville-Quincy Road) and the location of the trailer where Ted Weiher's body had been found (the Daniel Zink Campground), as shown on the map below.

As you will see on the map, if the Boys walked along the winding road, the distance they would have traveled would have been closer to 11 miles, not 19 miles. Of course, even walking 11 miles instead of 19 in those conditions would have been quite a feat and most likely would have taken the rest of the night and a good portion of the next day. I do not know what route the snowcat took to the trailer, but it has been reported that the snowcat followed the snow-covered Oroville-Quincy Highway until about a half-mile away from the trailer when the driver veered off the road to take a more direct route through the woods to the trailer. I cannot see how the Boys could have walked 19 miles unless they went in circles.

This information may help to explain part of this mystery: at least it explains how Gary Mathias and Ted Weiher, wearing only street clothes, made it through thick snow and high snowdrifts to get to the trailer. This error in reporting the distance between these two points is not surprising considering other misreported facts. Could it be law enforcement who parroted the account of the trailer's being 19 miles from where the car had been abandoned since they could not explain why they had failed to find a trailer that was really only 5.6 miles away (as the crow flies) from the car? That question will undoubtedly go unanswered as have so many others in this tragic case.

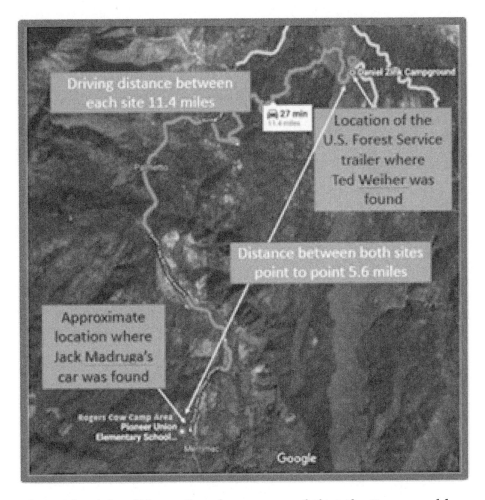

The authorities did say that they assumed that the Boys would go downhill, not uphill, in search of help.

Investigators speculated that either Mathias or Huett may have stayed in the trailer until Weiher died. Gary Mathias's tennis shoes were found in the trailer, and investigators believed that Mathias may have swapped his shoes for Ted Weiher's bigger, sturdier leather shoes as it is surmised that Mathias also had swollen frostbitten feet.

Each new finding was leading to new questions. What caused five grown men to go up that rural gravel mountain road and leave their car on a freezing cold night? Family members knew that despite the varying cognitive challenges each man had, the Boys simply would not get lost and stay lost.

As Jack Madruga's nephew George Madruga, who was 18 years old at the time his uncle went missing, told me:

> Those men were murdered by being forced or coerced to march to their ultimate demise from the elements. No way would Jack Madruga abandon his vehicle on the side of a mountain road without being forced or coerced to do so. He took an immense amount of pride in his car. Additionally, upon the off chance that he may have taken a wrong turn, he knew to simply turn around and retrace the route and not drive aimlessly until the road ended. Law enforcement did work the case, but I can't help but feel more could have been done. Just some "mentally challenged" Boys that got lost in the snow I believe was the final conclusion.

The newspaper reporters also played a major role in crafting the narrative that it was just some "retarded" Boys who got lost with headlines such as the June 19, 1978 *Los Angeles Times* article titled "Mystery of Retarded Men."

Jack's mother Melba also echoed the same sentiments as her grandson George Madruga had when she said:

> Things aren't right. They [the investigators] want to say they [the Boys] got stuck, walked out like a bunch of idiots and froze to death. Why would they leave the car to go die? There's no sense to that theory. But we can't figure anything that works out right, There's no rhyme

or reason to any of it.

Bill Sterling's sister Debby agreed that the Boys would not go up the Oroville-Quincy highway on their own accord. She stated:

> Someone made them go up that road. Bill didn't like the snow. They knew that it was cold up there. Madruga wouldn't have driven his car up there because he likes it too much.

Debby added that on one occasion, Jack Madruga had refused to take Jackie Huett home because the road to his house was too bad. (*The Sacramento Bee*, June 14, 1978.)

Right after the Boys disappeared, the families and investigators were entirely convinced foul play was involved. In the absence of answers from the investigators, the families became frustrated and were critical of how the investigation was handled.

"If we don't keep it in the news," said Bill Sterling's mother Juanita in a voice thick with emotion, "everybody will forget about it except us." (*The Sacramento Bee*, March 19, 1978)

In the March 19, 1978, *Sacramento Bee* Newspaper, Undersheriff Jack Beecham stated, "We're leaning toward the theory of an intervening force somewhere between Chico and the mountains, but we have absolutely no evidence to back that up."

About three weeks after the Boys went missing, a Yuba City woman named Debbie Lynn Reese, who is otherwise not known to have any connection to the case, picked up her telephone...

"Hello?" she said.

"I know where the missing five men are," a man on the other end of the line said before hanging up.

The man called back the next day and said, "I need help 'cause I really hurt those guys bad."

When she asked, "Who did you hurt?" he replied, "Don't play dumb with me," and hung up.

There was one more call the next day, on March 17.

"Those five guys are all dead," the man said.

'They're all dead?" Reese asked.

"They're all dead," he repeated.

Then the caller hung up, and Reese never heard from him again. (Gorney, 5 'Boys' Who Never Come Back, *The Washington Post*, July 6, 1978)

So many questions lingered.

It was speculated that the Boys did not eat much of the food available at the trailer camp because they were afraid of getting in trouble for stealing it and feared that the more food they "stole," the more trouble they would get into.

The fact that Ted Weiher did not attempt to make a fire seems very strange at first, but Ted was known to have trouble adapting to new situations. That still would not explain why Gary Mathias, if he indeed made to the trailer, would not have attempted to make a fire, turn on the gas to the trailer, or get more of the food from the other storage locker. Gary was the most intelligent of the group although he did suffer from schizophrenia.

According to the Mayo Clinic website, schizophrenia is a "serious mental disorder in which people interpret reality abnormally. Schizophrenia may result in some combination of hallucinations, delusions, and extremely disordered thinking and behavior that impairs daily functioning and can be disabling.

People with schizophrenia require lifelong treatment. Early treatment may help get symptoms under control before serious complications develop and may help improve the long-term outlook." (https://www.mayoclinic.org/diseases-conditions/ schizophrenia/ symptoms-causes/syc-20354443)

Gary had been prescribed three anti-psychotic drugs: Cogentin, Stelazine and Prolixin. Robert Pennock, the coach for the Boys' Gateway Gators Basketball team, told investigators that he felt that although Gary was medicated, he "could possibly flip out at any time." (*The Sacramento Bee,* Feb. 27, 2019.)

As Gary was the only man still missing, coupled with the facts that he was a late addition to the group and had a mental illness with a violent past, he became an immediate target of suspicion. Undersheriff Beecham told *The Sacramento Bee* in a 2019 article that at the time of the Boys' disappearance, several members of the families had told him personally that they had "deep concerns" that Gary was involved.

Dallas Weiher, Ted Weiher's brother, said that he believes that Mathias was involved in the other men's deaths and claims that Gary Mathias' family was the only one to turn down the show "Unsolved Mysteries" when the show's producers reached out to try to cover the case. Dallas said, "That's just suspicious. I'm not saying they knew, but well, you can probably guess what I think." (*The Sacramento Bee*, Febrary 27, 20190

As one would expect, the Mathias family did not share these concerns. Gary's sister, whom I interviewed for this book, told me that Gary seemed to tolerate his medications very well. She also told me that he had never had an outburst that she knew of and that his meds were set for him when he came back from Germany after he left the Army.

At some point after he came back from Germany, Gary was given a spiked drink at a party that resulted in his going out on the street and "acting high." When a police officer stopped Gary and tried to grab him, Gary got violent and was arrested. After the incident, Gary's mother Ida Marie Klopf, admitted him to a mental hospital, presumably at Gary's request. Gary was kept on the same pill regimen, but soon thereafter he was reevaluated by a new doctor who took him off the anti-psychotic drug Thorazine (Chlorpromazine), which had been causing him "high anxiety." Ida said that Gary's stepfather Bob Klopf religiously gave him his medications every day.

Although some of the families thought that Gary was involved in the disappearance, on the one-year anniversary of the Boys' disappearance, they all agreed to write an open letter to the editor in the *Midvalley Voices* section of the February 24, 1979, *Marysville Appeal Democrat*. This letter titled "Still One Missing, Still A Reward" appears to have been the idea of Robert "Bob" Klopf, the step-father of Gary Mathias, since he was the first person to add his name to it. The letter does have a heavy emphasis on the fact that Gary was still missing.

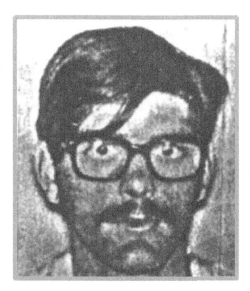

Gary Mathias

The most intriguing part of the letter is its criticism of the Butte

County Sherriff's Department for its refusal of the Forest Rangers' offer of help. The Rangers had offered to go to the trailer with snowmobiles in March.

The letter also states that it was falsely reported that Jack's car was stuck in the snow. It was not.

This letter further raises my personal suspicions that investigators may have played a part in repeating the narrative that the Boys walked nineteen miles to the trailer as a way to deflect criticism for their not finding the trailer, which was only 5.6 miles away from the abandoned car.

The open letter reads:

> Editor:
>
> Does it seem as long as a year ago, Feb. 24, 1978, when five young men (Ted Weiher, Bill Sterling, Jack Madruga, Jackie Huett and Gary Mathias) disappeared from our area? To all of the parents and families of each, it has been longer – a lifetime. Each of us has had our share of fear, pain, and sorrow, but we've also received a lot of sympathy and love from friends and even from people we've never had the opportunity to meet personally.
>
> Please let us again say "thank you" to all those people who gave of their time, work, and efforts for the recovery of the four that were found. Also, let this be a reminder to all that one, Gary Mathias, has never been located. Please, don't stop looking or let time dim your memories of the men who lived in your midst the majority of their lives. There is still a reward fund being held at a local bank and it will remain there until all five men are accounted for.
>
> A lot of questions have never been answered and possibly never will be. Why were they in the area where they were found? Was someone chasing them? Who was in the pickup seen parked behind the car? Why did they leave the car and wander off into snow when they could

have easily driven back down the same road they drove in on? The car was not stuck in the snow as was reported. They each had some problems, but stupidity certainly was not one of them. Why did the Butte County Sheriff's Department refuse the help of the forest rangers to go to the trailer camp with snowmobiles in March? At least one and maybe others may have been rescued at that time.

Questions, but no answers. Bitterness, some. Anger sometimes. Bewilderment, ALWAYS!

When your son leaves home with friends to go to a basketball game, do you always put your arms around him, give him a kiss and remind him how much you love him? You really should – he may never come back to you.

Robert L. Klopf
Ida M. Klopf
Imogene Weiher
Jack C. Huett
Sara M. Huett
Jim & Juanita Sterling

The sadness of that letter is palpable, but the sense of anger and frustration with the investigating authorities should not be overlooked.

CHAPTER 6: INQUISTION

E xactly forty years and two days would pass before any new information on the Yuba County Five case was reported in a two-part newspaper article printed in *The Sacramento Bee* Newspaper in 2019. The article was "Out in the Cold" by Bengy Egel.

The first part of the article, published on February 26, was subtitled "Four Mentally Disabled Men Died in The Woods. What Happened to The Fifth?" This section of the article gave good background information on the Boys and a summary of the case.

The second part of the article had the subtitle, "Were four mentally disabled men set up to die in the woods?" As there were actually five men who had gone missing in the woods, the subtitle of part two was a not-so-subtle hint that it was going to focus on the possibility that Gary Mathias was responsible for the death of his four friends.

Some previously unreported and underreported information pertaining to Gary Mathias's past, which came from police files to which the writer of the article was granted access, was presented in part two. There is no doubt that Gary was not like the other four Yuba County Boys. He is often referred to as the outlier of the group of five as he was not only relatively new to the group, but his handicap of having schizophrenia was not at all like the cognitive disability that the other four had. Gary did not have the sensitivity, shyness, and sometimes apparent vulnerability that the others had. Although Gary perhaps liked to think of himself as a "Fifth Shade" since that was the name of his band, some of the other Boys' family members said that they thought of him as more of a fifth wheel in his relationship with the four other Boys in the group.

The revelations about Gary in *The Sacramento Bee* article started with an incident during which he went on a "bad hallucinogenic trip" after taking illegal drugs while a sophomore in high school. The bad trip landed Gary in a psychiatric ward for a short period of time. Also mentioned was Gary's turbulent time in the Army, which included an AWOL arrest that led to Gary's calling two sergeants and a deputy over to his cell. When his cell was opened, a completely naked Gary walked into the hallway and punched one of the sergeants, causing blood to spill from his mouth and nose. Gary then attempted to punch the other sergeant but was quickly subdued before he was able to do so.

Gary was quoted at the time of the incident as saying "I've been in the Army, and I don't like it, and I thought that if I hit a cop, maybe they'd let me out." Gary was soon thereafter given a medical discharge from the Army for having schizophrenia.

The article also mentions a disturbing incident involving Gary that occurred just after he was released from the Army. One morning, Gary was watching T.V. at his cousin's house. After Gary's cousin realized that Gary had been taking an unusually long bathroom break, he went to check on him.

The cousin found him on top of his 17-year-old wife, groping her breasts while she was only wearing her underwear. She had been unable to alert her husband of the assault because she was very groggy from the medication she was taking to treat an ongoing illness.

When the cousin threatened to call 911 on him, Gary allegedly responded "Good, I want to go back to jail." Gary was charged with "assault with the attempt to rape" for this incident. According to The *Marysville Democrat* the "attempt to rape" charge was dropped as a result of a plea deal. Mathias did spend 8 months in jail for the assault charge.

Soon after he was released from jail, he was again in trouble with the law for doing hard drugs at the home of a couple he knew. The couple had reported that Mathias was acting erratically and talking about how he wanted to stab a woman in the jaw. He also allegedly told the couple's 3-year old daughter, "I thought I'd killed you once. I guess I'll do it again."

The woman's husband kicked Gary out of their house, and Gary banged on their locked door, trying to get back in, until the police arrived.

The Sacramento Bee article also listed other run-ins that Gary had with police, including "prowling at a cemetery" and a "slew of bar fights." Gary was undoubtedly a troubled person whose struggles with drugs and mental illness either were the cause of his actions or, at a minimum, made them much worse.

Please note that there has been some inconsistency in news reports of Mathias' run-ins with the law, and the chronology of events is sometimes unclear.

It was also mentioned that Gary had escaped from a mental hospital, to which he had been committed, by crawling through a drainpipe. Another dramatic story told of Gary's going to stay with his grandmother in Corvallis, Oregon, where she was the postmaster. After Gary was there for a few weeks, Gary's mother and stepfather pleaded with him to come home, but he hung up on them.

Five weeks later, Gary showed up on his parent's doorstep looking "ragged and filthy." Gary would explain that he had walked all the way from Corvallis, Oregon back to Marysville (536 highway miles), surviving on milk left on porches and dog food. According to Gary's sister, Tammie, Gary's grandmother had thrown him out.

The 2019 Sacramento Bee article did not present Gary Mathias in a good light. Mathias' niece reacted to *The Sacramento Bee* article's attempt to skewer Gary as follows:

> Gary Mathias was my uncle and his sister (the woman referred to in this article) was my mother. These articles are actually half-truths or skewed to paint a picture that just isn't true. They did not reach out to us or have permission to use my family's names either. They want to tarnish my uncle's character to have a

villain for their stories. I get it. We all want answers, but my uncle was not violent. He had a mental illness, yet he was sweet, quiet, artistic, and absolutely loved women and children.

There is a good explanation for all of these allegations recently put out about him and again you're only getting half-stories here. He was very close with my mom and his own mother was his best friend. Please have an open mind and remember his family does exist. All of them were on that mountain looking for him, including my father. These are memories that still haunt them.

Can you imagine never knowing what happened to your brother, son, or uncle for 40 years? Let me tell you; it's still painful. My family hasn't talked because it reopens wounds they don't want to revisit, so please have some compassion and understanding. I truly hope we all will learn the truth of what happened to my uncle Gary and his friends.

CHAPTER 7: VOICES OF THE FAMILIES

The Mathias Family

O
ne of the very first things that Gary's sister, Tammie, related to me was that nothing was ever going to bring Gary back and that discussing it "dredges up pain in her heart."

She also told me that she believes that people "drag on" Gary because he was never found.

Tammie went on to tell me of an unpleasant experience that Gary had had in Oregon, prior to staying with his grandmother, "Gary had gone to Oregon with some so-called friends. They locked him a closet for almost a month, fed him cat food; he broke loose, and hitchhiked it home in 2 days."

I asked her how Gary had gotten involved with the Gateway Projects as he had a mental illness and not an intellectual disability like the other Boys, and she replied:

> Gateway Projects was a place that disabled kids could go to for training. Help them to better themselves. Learn a job trade and help them to possibly live on their own. Gary went there at first for counselling and later was kept to help with the other guys. He showed them sports but also helped with other things they asked for. Gary also liked to help with maintenance too. The reason Gary had a blow up was he was being harassed by the druggers and such in our lousy town of Olivehurst. A lot was going on back then, naked to most eyes.

The blow-up she to which she referred was the last time Gary was arrested for disobeying a police officer after "acting high" on a public street. Tammie believes that Gary was intentionally given a "spiked" drink that caused him to have a bad reaction. That same evening Gary's mother admitted him to a mental hospital after he had asked her to do so. Tammie recalled that this particular incident happened about six months before Gary went missing.

She fully remembers Gary's run-ins with law enforcement since she was only a few years younger than he was.

Tammie also contends that Gary was doing very well in his new drug regimen and was excited about going to watch the basketball game in Chico and playing the next day in the Special Olympics tournament.

When I asked Tammie if she believed that Gary could have been responsible for what happened to the Boys, she told me:

> I know with all my heart that my brother took care of Ted [Weiher]. In the last possibly two weeks before Ted was found, he may have ventured out to get help, but I will never accept that he did anything wrong to his friends.

> Gary did not hurt those guys. Ted Weiher lived 13 weeks in that trailer, and someone took care of him. I know *Gary* did. I believe he had to watch all of his friends die before he left on foot to find his own confused mind a way out. He would have contacted one of us if he had been alive himself. It's been 42 years and my tears keep flowing like it was yesterday.

She also told me that she is the only immediate family member of Gary's who is still alive. Sadly, Gary and Tammie's sister, Sharon, committed suicide in 2002. It has been speculated that she may have had some form of depression or mental illness that contributed to her suicide. Gary's biological father, Garland had also committed suicide in 1997.

Sharon Lavonne Mathias

Gary's mother Ida had a turbulent relationship with Gary's father. When Gary was only 3 years old, his mother fled from his father, making it all the way to Bakersfield before she had a change of heart and called Garland to come and pick them up. Some years later, Ida left Garland for good and got a restraining order against him.

Gary's brother-in-law, Gary Whiteley, who had been married to Gary's sister Sharon and was going through a divorce with her at the time the Boys went missing, was quoted in the previously-mentioned 2019 *Sacramento Bee* article, saying that drugs had "warped Mathias' brain" and that "he was not mentally stable." Tammie told me that Whiteley's relationship with her was highly volatile and was cause for many calls to the local police. In fact, Whiteley had a turbulent relationship with the entire family. It was also reported that Whiteley himself was no stranger to drugs and assaulting people. In fact, according to Tammie, Whiteley had once burned her mother's car to the ground.

Whiteley had served in combat in Vietnam and had reconnected with Gary Mathias after Gary had returned from his military service in Germany.

Gary's mother and his stepfather continued to receive Gary's military disability pay and social security payments for seven years after Gary had gone missing. After they were forced to declare that Gary was dead for legal reasons, they had to pay back the majority of the money because they had spent it all. It had been kept in an account at a Marysville bank.

The Brawl at Behr's Market

I asked Tammie what she thinks caused the Boys to be found on that mountain, and she first said that it may have been the result of a brawl that had happened in the parking lot of Behr's market. She said that the brawl was reported to Lt. Ayres by a man related to the store owner.

Tammie said that the Mathias family was told by Ayres that a group of men approached Jackie Huett in the parking lot of the store and started taunting him. Gary Mathias was said to have jumped in to defend Jackie, and a larger fight broke out between Gary and the group taunting Jackie Huett. Gary would have been the only one out of his group that would have been able to (or know how to) defend himself.

Tammie said that she had heard that the brawl was broken up by the store clerk. I assume that she means the store clerk Mary Davis, but she does not know for sure. I was not able to find any news report substantiating that any fight took place at Behr's.

Many years later, a woman claiming to be Jackie Huett's sisters-in-law posted on a true crime blog that she believed that there was a fight at Behr's market and that the men who started the fight possibly chased the Boys after leaving the store, causing them to become lost.

It has been written that Ted Weiher's sister believed that there was a brawl/altercation at Behr's market or after the game. Jackie Huett's sister-in-law also believes that the brawl occurred. (*The*

Sacramento Bee, June 14, 1978.)

Tammie also told me of a time that she thought she had seen her Gary, long after he had disappeared, when she was working as a nurse at a hospital. Being a nurse was the kind of work that was exhausting with long days and frustrating when doctors (and patients) didn't listen, but it was also fulfilling to care for people, to ease their pain, and to help them to heal. The first month or two after Gary's disappearance, Tammie had struggled to work and had even taken a few weeks off, but now she found that work was really the only place where she could forget, well almost forget, what had happened.

Sometimes she would catch herself wondering if Gary were still alive, maybe in a hospital somewhere, with a nurse taking care of him the way she took care of her patients. She prayed that someone was taking good care of Gary even though she believed deep down that he was no longer living.

Tammie had never really been a clock-watcher, and usually her days at work were so busy that she seldom had time to even glance at her watch, but today had felt like it would never end. Just two hours to go. Two hours and then dinner and sleep, not necessarily in that order. Two hours to go. 6:00 pm. Time to give Mrs. Edwards in Room 212 her pain meds. Time to see if Miss Borden in Room 215 had been able to keep any of her dinner down. Time for stopping by Room 218 to listen to old Mr. DiMaggio's baseball stories. Of course, he wasn't *that* Mr. DiMaggio, but he actually had played professional baseball, and he was a kind man who needed company.

"I don't think he's had one visitor since he got here three days ago," Tammie said to herself. "I will stop in and chat with him as soon as I check on the new patient in Room 220."

With that thought, Tammie finished the rest of her coffee and started down the hallway. Room 220 was at the very end of the hall. She would start at the far end and work her way down, checking in on each patient, finally ending up at the nurses' station, where she would have another cup of coffee and wait for her relief to show up.

It took only a couple of minutes for Tammie to get to room 220. She did her best to be cheerful and walked into the room, smiling, and saying, "Hi. How are you feeling? I am your nurse, Tammie. Is there anything you need?"

She glanced over at the bed and saw a young man lying there, his left arm in a sling. She bent down to pull his chart from the holder at the foot of the bed when she felt compelled to look at him again. When she looked up, she dropped his chart on the floor. The young man was Gary!

Stunned, Tammie stared at him for a moment, not even bothering to pick up the clipboard and papers that she had dropped on the floor.

The young man broke the spell she was under by answering the questions that she had forgotten she had asked.

"I don't feel too bad," he said. "In some pain. Can I get something for that?"

He sounded like Gary, too!

Tammie put her hands along the top of her head to keep her brain from exploding out of her skull. "Gary! Gary!" This can't be Gary!" she said to herself. To the young man, she said, "What is your name?"

"Gary," he replied.

"Gary! Your name is Gary!" Tammie's head was spinning, and she felt herself starting to faint, so she held onto the bed's footboard to prop herself up. "Gary Mathias?"

"Gary Anderson," he responded.

"Maybe Gary has lost his memory and is using another name," she thought. "Where do you come from? How did you end up here?" she asked.

"I was in a car wreck on Arboga Road," he replied. Then, noticing that his nurse was staring at him strangely, he asked, "Is something wrong? Are you okay?"

"Uh, yeah, sure," Tammie answered as she attempted to pull herself together and pick up the mess she had made on the floor. "Do you know a man named Gary Mathias?" she asked.

He looked at her and waited a moment to answer.

"He is wondering why I am acting so weirdy," Tammie said to herself. To her patient, she said, "Gary Mathias is my brother. Do you know him?"

"Nope," he replied. "I don't know him."

"You, you look just like him, and you talk like him, too. Are you sure - does the name sound familiar?" she asked pleadingly.

She was trying to *will* him to say, "Yes." To say that he had not known who he was for a while but hearing the name Gary Mathias had jarred his memory, and that yes, he was Gary Mathias, her brother whom she loved, her long-lost brother who had now returned home.

But he did not say that. Instead, he said, his irritation evident, "Yes, I am sure that I don't know him. Could you please see about getting me something for my pain?"

That question thrust her back into reality - the reality that Gary was gone and the reality that she had a job to do – and she pulled herself together as best she could and went to the nurse's station to submit a request for a doctor's signature for Demerol for the patient in Room 220.

At the nurses' station she asked the staff if they knew anything about the guy in 220. They did not know much more than she did.

Gary Anderson, age 28, had been in a car accident and would be staying for a few days.

Tammie wanted to tell them that he looked just like her Gary, but then she thought better of it. She was afraid that if she said something, she might somehow jinx something - although she was not sure what that something was.

For the rest of her shift, the same thought kept going through her head. *Even though the man in 220 looks and sounds like my Gary, exactly like my Gary, he couldn't be my Gary. But he looks and sounds like my Gary, exactly like my Gary, so he has to be my Gary.*

Tammie left the hospital that night, shocked that someone could seem so much like Gary, yet not be Gary. "Perhaps, it's just wishful thinking," she told herself. "Maybe he doesn't resemble Gary as much as I think he does. I will sleep on it. Maybe when I see him tomorrow, he will not look as much like Gary as he did tonight."

The next day, Tammie returned to the hospital, still a little shaken from the events of the day before but determined to be sensible. The first patient she decided to check on was the man in 220. As she walked down the hall to room 220, she told herself, "Keep it together, Tammie. Maybe today he won't look so much like Gary." And she bowed her head a little and asked God to help her as she walked through the doorway and into the room.

Once in the room, she lifted her head up and said, "Good morning. How are you feeling today?" But there was no answer because there was no one in the room! Stunned, Tammie checked the door number to see if she was in the right room. She was. She checked the bathroom, even though the door was open, and it was obvious that no one was in there. Surprised, she went to the nurses' station and asked what had happened to the man in 220.

"Someone checked him out late last night," was the reply from the Head Nurse.

"I thought he was going to be here for a few days," said Tammie.

"He was," the Head Nurse responded without any apparent concern. "But someone checked him out last night. His father, I think. Go figure."

Tammie did not understand any of it. It was another mystery added to the many mysteries surrounding Gary.

Although Gary Mathias' family has been absent from the media in recent years, On February 24th, 2008, on the 30-year anniversary of Gary's disappearance, they ran the following obituary in the *Marysville Appeal Democrat*.

Gary Mathias
October 15, 1952 - February 24, 1978

Part of us, yet parted from us.
Managing grief that becomes us.
Departed in body; eternal in thought
Birthday gifts no longer bought.
Gone to the Heaven far above us
Parted from us, forever far from us.

Love Always
Mark and Lavelle Mathias
And Sons

The Huett Family

I had contacted Jackie Huett's sister-in-law, Mary, to see what her account of the Behr's Market brawl was, but she did not wish to comment on anything relating to the Yuba County Five. I did make contract with Mary's daughter-in-law, Brandy, who was very accommodating and was able to get many of my written questions for the Huett family answered by Jackie Huett's younger brother, David.

My first question was if the Huett family believed that Gary Mathias was responsible for the disappearance of the Yuba County Five.

The exact response I received was "No, we [the Huett family] do not believe Gary Mathias was involved."

I also asked about an internet post made by a woman named Jessica, who claimed to be a relative of Gary Mathias. (I was later able to verify that "Jessica" is related to Gary Mathias.) She wrote that she believed that a local man, who is still living in the Marysville area, was responsible for the Boys' disappearance. Jessica further stated that there was a lot that the public did not know about the case. Of course, many people responded to her claim and asked her to reveal the name of the person she believed was responsible for the Boys' disappearance, but she did not respond back.

A crime blogger from the Yuba City area did respond on the same message thread claiming that she knew who this individual was and that it could not be revealed as "they" still live in the community and are somewhat prominent. I was able to make contact with the local blogger and asked about that person in general terms.

I was surprised that I was quickly given the name of the suspected individual. I did not ask for the name, I only wanted to know what the genesis of the claim was and what possible motive to harm the Boys this individual would have had. The blogger told me that the suspected individual had a bad history with Gary Mathias, a history going back several years, and had made threats against him in the past.

Now that I had the name of a person of interest, whose identity I will not reveal – except to say that at some later point, "they" became a pastor - I was able to verify that this man did know Gary Mathias and his family very well. I was also able to verify that this man had an extensive criminal record involving drugs and violence. From all appearances, this person turned "their" life around in the 1980s and has had no further problems with law enforcement.

I asked Cathy what her thoughts were on the person of interest who had been named by a member of her family, and she said that she knew this person of interest very well and that it was highly likely that "they" were involved.

She also said that many people with whom Gary was social knew that he was planning to go to the basketball game in Chico that fateful Friday night and that may have presented an opportunity for a person or group of persons to plan some sort of attack on Gary Mathias.

The main points that the Mathias family and the Huett family seem to agree on is that Gary Mathias was not responsible for what happened and that the Boys were targeted by another group, somehow causing them to wind up on that cold road, halfway up a mountain, in the Plumas National Forest.

This is the most important question that I asked Brandy to pose to David Huett: *Has David ever heard that what happened to the Boys was caused by someone who lived (and possibly still lives) in the Yuba City area and was angry with Gary Mathias?*

David Huett's response was, "Yes. Someone locally did this. We cannot disclose any names as he's a pastor. We all know the name of who did this." Another Huett family member has referred to this pastor as the town bully. It should be noted that at the time of the Boys' disappearance and death, this man of whom they speak was not yet a pastor.

I also asked if David had ever heard that gun shell casings had been found by Jack Madruga's abandoned car. I had read that somewhere, but did not find it in newspaper reports, so I assumed that it was most likely an internet rumor. I was surprised when he responded, "Yes. There were gun shells, firing a gun into or at the Boys, believed to scare the Boys so they'd run."

1. Marysville, where the Boys lived
2. Chico, where the basketball game was held
3. Where the 4 Boys' bodies were found
4. Where the Boys' car was abandoned
5. Oroville Dam

David Huett has stated, "Gary Mathias was thrown over the Oroville Dam, so his body would never be found."

Although David would not disclose the name of the pastor that he suspected of this crime, his statement did seem to confirm the statement made by the blogger with whom I had been communicating - the statement that the person responsible for what had happened to the Boys later became a pastor.

I also asked Gary's sister Tammie about the possibility that her brother had been thrown over the Oroville Dam, and she said that she was very familiar with that rumor, but "if Gary were thrown over the dam, there would not have been any evidence that Gary was ever in the trailer." It was reported by police that Gary's shoes were left in the trailer, and Tammie added that she actually went to the Forest Service trailer herself and found some handwritten notes that belonged to Gary, scraps of paper that had something similar to journal writing on them.

She told me, "Gary took notes to himself like a diary. And several of the writings were found inside, and it was checked by a specialist on writing. They matched Gary's handwriting. They only claimed that a few of the GI rations were used. I saw a lot more. Jack Madruga and Gary were the only two to know military survival. Jack died before they made it to the trailer. That left my Gary."

I was not able to find any other account of Gary Mathias leaving notes in the service trailer.

Tammie said that the notes contained only religious passages and affirmations of encouraging words about getting through tough circumstances and did not contain anything pertaining to what may have caused the Boys to abandon their car and head uphill in the freezing darkness. The police took the pieces of paper and never returned them to her.

Tammie believes that the story of Gary's being thrown over the Oroville dam, which is over an hour south of where Jack Madruga's car was abandoned, came from a man named Alan Martin, who stopped by the Mathias home a few months after the Boys' bodies were found and told the family that he had been with a group of men that had stopped the Boys on the bridge near the Oroville Dam. One of the men "started slapping Jackie Huett to hear him whine." It was known that Jackie would start to make a guttural whining sound when he was distressed.

Alan stated that Gary became angered by Jackie's being slapped and jumped on the man that slapped him, beating him up. In turn, the other men jumped on Gary. Tammie did not recall if Alan said that Gary had been thrown over the bridge. She did recollect that Alan claimed that Glen Baker was the person who, after this fight, drove Jack Madruga's car up the mountain road to where it was abandoned, near the Rogers Cow Camp campground. Tammie believes that Alan told the story to the Mathias family out of guilt.

It is not known if Alan Martin ever went to the police with his story, but it is known that Ida Klopf reported Alan's story to Deputy Lance Ayres. Unfortunately, Deputy Ayres was not able to question Alan Martin because Martin died two days after he had visited Gary Mathias' family. Martin died under rather suspicious circumstances, found dead of a heroin overdose on a couch in his friends Carl and Anna Gage's home. Martin was a known pill popper but had never been known to use heroin.

Tammie said that she assumes that when the car was driven up the road, the Boys were all inside. She believes that at some point, the car was stopped along the Oroville-Quincy Highway, and the boys were ordered to get out of the car. Once out of the car, the Boys were threatened or frightened by someone, and they took off running into the freezing woods. Perhaps they had witnessed Gary's murder and had seen his body being thrown over the dam. She said that her family hired a diver to search Lake Oroville based on the story told by Alan, but no sign of Gary was ever found. For over twenty-five years after his disappearance, Tammie would "throw flowers into Oroville Lake" in remembrance of her brother.

Tammie also added that one of the men that she believes was part of the group of men who was with Alan and the still-living person of interest, was a man that drove a red step-side truck. She thinks that the red truck could be the one later reported by Joe Schons. According to Tammie, soon after Alan had come by their house, he died mysteriously, and the man who owned the red truck moved to Arizona soon thereafter. I asked her to elaborate on how Alan had died, and she told me the following:

> He [Alan] was brought over to Carl Gage's house as they thought he had just passed out. They put him on their couch and left. Anna checked on him the next morning, and he was blue, so they called 911. He apparently died of a drug overdose by injection. Alan never ever shot up, only dropped pills, so him having a bad overdose from an injection was highly suspicious. Alan's girlfriend said some guys took him out of the house, and she never saw him alive again. It remains unclear if an ambulance ever showed up and took him to a hospital, or if the men took him to the hospital or somewhere else.

I told Tammie that I had read that part of the reason that Gary was suspected of having some involvement with the disappearance of the Boys was that it was said that her family had refused to be interviewed by the television show *Unsolved Mysteries*. Many of the popular YouTube uploads about the Yuba County Five case mention this and state that the Mathias family was the only family out of the five families that refused to participate in the show, thus causing the show to choose not to do the episode. She said that my telling her about it was the first time she ever heard of it. She said she was a fan of the show and that the family would have loved to have had national media involved to help in the search for Gary and to provide new leads in the case. She said her mother never mentioned the show contacting her. That was one of the many unsubstantiated stories of the Yuba County Five case that still linger on after all these years.

The Weiher and Sterling Families

I reached out to Weiher and Sterling family members, but they politely declined to comment. I, of course, respect their wishes not to discuss the case.

Ted Weiher's sister-in-law has theorized that the men may have seen something take place at the basketball game that prompted someone to chase them. *(The Washington Post,* July 6, 1978)

Police were never able to establish evidence for a pursuit, but no one could shake the idea that the men seemed to be determined to move forward up the cold, dark mountain. Why would they do that unless something more frightening was right behind them? George Madruga told me that although his uncle Jack Madruga did not know the road that his prized Montego was found on, he was confident that Jack could drive well on poorly maintained roads, driving carefully so that his car would not be damaged. "Uncle Doc [Jack Madruga] could negotiate such a road easily. My grandmother and he lived in a house on a rutted dirt road approximately one-half mile or more from the main road. He drove such a road nearly every day!"

The Madruga Family

As far as Jack Madruga's family is concerned, Gary Mathias is still very suspect in the disappearance of the Boys.

Jack's nephew George Madruga told me that his family "believed all along that he [Mathias] was the key to this whole mystery. I totally believe that he was involved one way or another."

He added the bombshell story that his sister, who had met Gary Mathias on several occasions, firmly believes she saw him at some point after the Boys disappeared. She had met Gary Mathias more than a few times and knew exactly what he looked like.

The members of the Madruga family had always been very close, and they grew even closer after the tragedy. Haunted by what-ifs, lost chances, second guesses, and never-beens, Grandma Melba, Cathy, her parents, and Aunt Janet leaned on each other for support and sought comfort in each other's presence. Doc was always in their hearts and always on their minds, but, of course, the work of living had to be done and the minutiae of everyday existence forced the tragedy (out of necessity) into the compartment of their minds labeled, The Past, and they all functioned as best they could, most of the time more half-dead than half-alive. The Past, though, has a habit of intruding itself onto the present, often when it is least expected, and the past slammed into Cathy one evening in a way that she had never anticipated.

Cathy had just finished a long day of work for the forestry service and had started her drive home when she realized that she did not really want to be by herself all evening and decided to stop in at her parents' bar and grill, La Casa Blanca. She could grab something to eat there and seeing her mother would take away, at least temporarily, some of the emptiness that constantly filled her heart.

Since Doc had gone, Cathy's sense of security, the foundation of a world in which things were orderly and questions had answers, had evaporated, and Cathy felt like a ship on a churning sea, a ship that could capsize at any moment. Cathy's parents were still here, thank God! But they could be taken away at any moment and knowing this, not just with her mind (as we all know), but knowing this, since Doc's passing, with every fiber of her being had the effect of making the anticipation nearly as bad as the event itself and had left Cathy feeling entirely alone if she did not keep herself busy.

The drive to La Casa Blanca was not long, but Cathy felt a sense of relief as she pulled into the parking lot. The glow of the neon lights in the twilight of the day gave her the sense of comfort that only warm childhood memories can bring. "Stopping here was a good idea," she said to herself as she parked behind the building, next to her mom's green Cutlass. The parking lot was more than half full.

"Business must be pretty good; that means that Mom will be in a good mood," Cathy thought to herself as she walked along the side of the building, turned to the left, and walked up wide steps that led to a rather elegant-looking front porch, a holdover from when the building was a private residence. In fact, the building was still a private residence, with Cathy's parents living upstairs and running the bar downstairs.

As Cathy took her first step onto the porch, she felt the familiar, slightly spongy, creaky feel of the porch floorboards, boards that had to be at least 75 years old and probably needed to be replaced soon. She walked across the porch a couple of times, checking to see if any of the boards seemed loose or rotting. Satisfied that the porch was safe for now, it was time go inside, and, she headed for the heavy wooden door, which looked like it had come from an old sailing ship and didn't seem to go with the crisp whiteness of the rest of the building. The door was flanked by a Miller High Life sign glowing in the window on the left and a Pabst Blue Ribbon sign in the window on the right. As a girl, Cathy had wondered exactly what "High Life" was. She still wasn't really sure what it was, but she was pretty sure that she had never experienced it. She had always liked the blue ribbon on the Pabst Blue Ribbon sign. It reminded her of the time that she had dressed up as a pink bunny rabbit for Halloween at school and had won the blue ribbon for prettiest costume.

Even before opening the door, Cathy could smell cigarette smoke and hear Buck Owens on the jukebox. The music was a little louder and the smoke was a lot thicker when she walked in, forcing her to squint to keep her eyes from burning.

"Thank heaven, some things never change," she said to herself as she made her way between the bar on her right and the tables with the checkerboard tops on her left.

Directly in the back, past the bar, first door on the right was the ladies' room, and that's where she was headed. She noticed that practically every bar stool was taken and most of the tables were, too. "Must be the special is good tonight," she thought, and she saw that there were even a couple of children at the Casa, sitting with their parents at a table near the jukebox.

The ladies' room was just as it always was, kind of an afterthought, with hot water that never really got hot and a towel dispenser than never really worked. At least it was clean. One thing about her mother, she always kept the place clean. Cathy dried her hands on her work pants and walked out into the smoke and the sounds of people enjoying the evening.

She thought about the last real birthday party that she had had here. It seemed like so long ago. That was her last birthday party that Doc had been to. He had given her a little wooden jewelry box that he had made at the Gateway Projects. He had felt so bad when the music box part did not work after he had wound it too far. Cathy did not care that the music did not play; she loved the jewelry box anyway because Doc had made it for her, made it for her with love.

She was thinking about how things, like people, don't have to be perfect to be loveable when she glanced over at the bar, and she saw a man she recognized. He was sitting on a barstool, third one from the door, and he was looking directly at her. Her eyes met his, and she knew. She *knew*. It was Gary Mathias!

"Gary Mathias!" she shouted without even realizing it, and she rushed back into the kitchen, behind the bar, to tell her parents.

"Mom, Gary Mathia is out there, at the bar. It's him! It's him! It's him! I know it's him!" Cathy exclaimed as she walked through the gray double doors that led into the kitchen, shaking with excitement, anger, and other emotions that she could not even identify as she startled her mother, who standing at the grill.

"Call the cops!" Cathy's mom's voice trembled as she pointed to the phone with a spatula, dripping grease onto the floor.

Cathy instantly grabbed the phone while her mother asked, "Where is he? Where is he?"

"He's sitting at the bar, third stool from the door. It's him! It's him!" Cathy said as calmly as she could while she dialed the number to the sheriff's office.

Cathy had called the sheriff's office so many times that she knew the number by heart. Cathy's mother sprinted to the bar area with Cathy following her a couple of minutes later after a deputy had promised to be right over. But there was nobody sitting at the third barstool from the door. Gary had gone.

Immediately Cathy and her mother asked the patrons if they had seen the man leave, if they knew what he had driven, if they knew who he was. Nobody knew anything. They even asked a male regular to check in the men's room to see if anybody was in there. They searched the whole place, inside and outside, even the living quarters. But the man was gone. Gary was gone. And nobody knew where he went.

When the deputy finally showed up, which was only about 15 minutes after Cathy had placed her call, he was met with two distraught and dejected women, one of whom was determined to convince him that Gary Mathias was still alive and needed to be brought in for questioning. The Deputy was familiar with the Yuba County Five case, and he listened patiently as Cathy explained what had happened. The following day, the sheriff arranged a photo lineup and asked Cathy to pick out the man whom she had seen at the bar the day before. The photo she chose was a photo of Gary Mathias.

Cathy's sighting of Gary Mathias brought the Madruga family hope that finally they might get some answers, but as the weeks, months, and years went by, their hope gradually faded until it all but disappeared. To this day, Cathy insists that the man she saw at La Casa Blanca was Gary Mathias.

Gary Mathias

The Madruga family was not pleased with the effort put forth by law enforcement during its investigation of what had happened to the Boys (the Forest Service trailer and Jack's car were never even fingerprinted), so Cathy's aunt Janet did some investigating on her own. Aunt Janet was able to determine (to her satisfaction) who was responsible for the death of her brother, and roughly 10 years after the Boys' disappearance, she arranged to confront this man one evening at a Marysville restaurant. About six months before Janet's death in 2018, she relayed to Cathy what had transpired during this meeting. Janet told her that as she got ready for her meeting with Doc's killer, she was so filled with emotion that her hands were practically shaking as she took the Saturday night special she had inherited from her grandfather out of the nightstand drawer.

"I've got to pull myself together," she thought as she popped open the cylinder to make sure that there was a round in each chamber. Janet had a habit of keeping only four rounds in the revolver, leaving an empty chamber lined up with the barrel to prevent her from accidentally firing it. Tonight, though, Janet had no worry of an accidental shooting. Tonight's shooting would be intentional.

Firearm fully loaded, Janet slipped it into a small empty purse, figuring that if she had to, she could easily shoot through the purse. She hoped it would not come to that. She much preferred the idea of pulling out the firearm and watching Doc's murderer squirm, possibly begging for his life, before she sent him on his final journey, a journey that no doubt would lead to the gates of Hell.

Janet had never wanted to kill anyone or anything in her life. There is a member of every family who takes in stray dogs and cats, who won't step on a spider, who feels guilty swatting at mosquitos. Janet was this member of the Madruga family. But sometimes in life, there is a momentous occasion that changes the way a person responds to the world, that changes the calling of a person's heart; a time when everyday thoughts, feelings, desires, and dreams fade into the background, and the truly important things, the ideals that separate us from the animals - justice, freedom, love, faith - come to the forefront and are the only things that matter. Janet had reached that point. Tonight, Janet would carry out justice for her beloved brother Doc. God, after all, was a God of justice. Sure, He was a God of mercy, but ultimately, He was a God of justice. That is why there is a Judgment Day. And today would be Doc's killer's earthly judgment day. And Janet would be his judge, jury, and executioner.

Janet put her wallet and a small notepad, which contained all of the information that she had gathered in her quest to find out why

Doc had been killed, in her jacket pocket and buttoned the pocket closed. Janet never went anywhere without her little notebook; it was precious to her. As she grabbed her keys, started her car, and drove to the restaurant, she felt the adrenaline rise within her, and she prayed that she would be strong enough to do what she knew she had to do.

It took Janet about 20 minutes to get to the restaurant, but she had planned on the trip talking twice as long, so she went inside, got a table for two, and ordered a drink. She was about halfway through her scotch and soda when Doc's killer arrived. Janet had told him that she would be wearing a blue cotton barn coat, and it appeared that he did not have any trouble recognizing her as he stood at the front of the dining area for only a minute before he began to walk to her table.

Janet could feel her heart beating fast as he said, "You must be Janet," and he sat down after Janet nodded her head.

Janet had gone over in her head a million times what she would say to him when she finally met him, but now words seemed to fail her and she remained quiet for a moment, just looking at him.

The man broke the silence. "You said you wanted to talk to me – in person. Well, here I am. I don't know what you . . ."

Janet interrupted him and got right to the point. "I know you are responsible for killing my brother. And the other Boys." She was filled with emotion, but her blood ran as cold as ice, and her voice was strong and determined. Her eyes looked directly into his, and she gave him a second to process what she had just said while she unzipped the purse on her lap and felt around for the rubbery grip of her gun.

"You know why I am here," she said matter-of-factly. "I am going to kill you."

The man pushed his chair back from the table and began to speak, but Janet did not hear a word he said because God began speaking to her at the same time.

The Lord's words were few but powerful. "Two wrongs don't make a right. Put the gun down."

God's voice echoed throughout her body. Janet could do nothing but obey, and she released the grip on her pistol and let it fall back into its resting place in her purse as she watched the man run out of the restaurant, yelling something about getting away from a crazy woman.

Janet did not really remember much about the rest of the night. She somehow made it home, dazed and unsteady, put her revolver back in the drawer where it belonged, and slept the deepest sleep she had in years, still haunted by the specter of sorrow but no longer tormented by the revenant of revenge.

Jack Madruga

Cathy was shocked by her aunt's story – not so much by the fact that her aunt had told her that she was going to kill the man she believed had killed her brother, but by that fact that her aunt had told her that this man, the man who may have killed her uncle, would go on to become pastor.

When Cathy told me over the phone that the man her Aunt Janet believed was responsible for the death of her brother and his friends had become a pastor at some point later in his life, I felt my heart stop – I thought that this perplexing case may finally be close to getting solved!

I calmly, but excitedly, asked her, "Did your aunt give you the name of the man she thought was responsible for the deaths of the Boys?"

It felt like an eternity but must have only been a second before she responded, "Yes, she did."

Before she had even finished saying the word "Yes," I practically shouted, "What was his name?"

I fully expected to hear the same name that the Yuba County blogger had given me, the name of the man who had in later life become a pastor, the name of the man who seemed more and more suspicious as I conducted more and more research. I could feel that kind of excitement that only comes from being on the verge of discovering something big. My heart, which held felt like it had stopped at the beginning of our conversation, was now racing, and I felt like I was floating in the clouds.

Then Cathy's words brought me back down to earth.

Cathy game me a different name entirely!

I was stunned.

I had never divulged to Cathy the name of the man who was suspected by a number of people, including the Huett family, of causing the Boys' disappearance and deaths, so she had no idea how let down I was at the moment she had given me a different name. But how could this be? How many killers-turned-pastors could be running around Yuba County, California?

The name she revealed did not seem very common, so I asked

Cathy if she had ever heard of this man before her aunt had mentioned him. She replied that when she was a child growing up in Marysville, there was someone with that name who lived nearby, but she didn't know the man well.

After I got off the phone with Cathy, I got in touch with Gary Mathias's sister Tammie and asked her if she had heard of the man that Janet had revealed to Cathy.

Cathy immediately replied, "Of course, I have. I just talked to his sister last week. He died just a few months ago."

Again, I was stunned.

I then asked her, "Was this man ever a pastor?"

She replied, "No. He was always in construction as far as I know. He knew Gary well. He and Gary ran around with a group of friends in the '70's after Gary returned from Germany."

Cathy paused for a moment, trying to dig up memories from a time that she would rather forget. She then added that that this man also knew the original suspect who later became a pastor.

Again, I was stunned.

I quickly asked her if these two men were friends, and she responded that they were not. She said that the original suspect did not have any friends, but that some people hung around him out of plain fear.

"He was the kind of person that people just didn't say no to," Cathy added, "He just got his way."

"How could both of these men know each other and somehow not be connected to the disappearance of the Boys?" I wondered to myself. "Could it be possible that Cathy's Aunt Janet had given her the wrong name to protect her?"

I then thought that it was much more likely that Janet was correct in thinking that the man who had murdered her brother had became a pastor later in life, but she had somehow gotten his name wrong. Maybe the second man, the man who had not become a pastor, had been with the group of men (which included Glen Baker and Alan Martin) that had allegedly thrown Gary over the dam.

It could also be possible that by the time Janet learned of the Boys' being victims of foul play, the story may have been far less than accurate since it had been repeated so many times over the years by the Boys' family members and curious locals. Tammie did not know any of Jack Madruga's family, so it is not too surprising that that they recalled different versions of basically the same story.

Just when I thought the story of the Yuba County Five could get not any stranger, Tammie told me that the 12-year-old brother of the man that Janet had revealed as the Boy's killer was brutally murdered in 1975. His killer was never caught.

Tammie added that some of the man's family members felt that the original suspect-turned-pastor was the murderer of the boy, who had been killed while swimming alone at a watering hole. He and his sister had skipped school one day to go swimming with a group of friends. His sister and his friends left the swimming hole before he did, and it is presumed that a man showed up and assaulted and murdered the boy once he was alone. That case is still unsolved.

The ancillary tragedies that surround the Yuba County Five case were becoming almost as strange as the original disappearance to me. But were any of them related to what had happened to the Yuba County Five?

Jack Madruga, Vietnam ca. 1968

Jack Madruga's mother, Melba, passed away just a few months after Jack's body was found. As George Madruga puts it, "It seemed like she fairly lost her will to go on. I would say that she died of a broken heart, for she was never the same after this."

Cathy also told me of something that she has regretted for over 40 years. Shortly before the Boys went missing, Cathy had been living in Fresno. Doc called her one evening and asked if he could bring some friends over for the weekend. Cathy was tired and she did not want to deal with a house full of young men, so she told him, "No," to which he replied in a joking way, "What, you don't like me?"

Cathy knew that she would see Doc sooner or later, so she remained firm in her denial.

It was the last time that she would ever speak to him.

CHAPTER 8: WHO WAS JOSEPH SCHONS?

J oseph Schons, (often misspelled as Shones in media reports about this case) was 55 years old at the time the Yuba County Boys went missing and lived on a dirt road called Schons Road in Berry Creek. As explained to me by one of Joe Schons former neighbors, whom I will refer to as "Todd" as he wishes to remain anonymous, Schons lived on mountain acreage about a mile north of Rockefeller Road. Todd went on to tell me that Schons, along with his wife and daughter, arrived in the Berry Creek area not long before Todd had, which he estimated to be sometime in 1977 when Todd was living with his cousin and his cousin's wife. He described Schons physically as "an older guy, pretty tall at least 6 feet, with grey curly hair, big grey mustache, big beer belly, kind of looked like Fat Freddy from the Freak Brothers comics."

I was able to independently verify much of the information that Todd gave me, and I determined that Todd was very credible.

Todd also told me that "He (Schons) used to drive around all day, drinking beers, to get away from his wife. Everyone who lived in the area would see his vehicle stuck, and we often winched it free of whatever ditch it was in. If he caught us fixing our awful road, he'd bend our ears with bullshit stories and bad advice. He had angina, and often mentioned he had heart trouble. He seemed harmless, but we did track down some wild rumors that originated with him and his wife."

Todd personally felt that Schons was harmless, but he had heard many wild rumors that originated from Schons and his wife. Todd had been busy working at the time that the Yuba Boys disappeared, so he didn't hear about the incident until long after it happened.

Todd said that as time went by, the Schonses managed to alienate a number of the locals with their harmful gossip, by not paying people they had hired, and by their generally unfriendly and downright mean behavior.

"Drunk or sober, Schons just could not tell the truth about anything

and was a blowhard that rubbed a lot of people the wrong way."

Todd further elaborated about Schons' propensity not to tell the truth:

> Schons used to tell wild bullshit stories, to guys that were former military, like myself, and to real combat veterans that we knew. He was the same age as my Dad, which meant he was 16 in 1945, but he'd insist he parachuted onto Guadalcanal as a Marine Raider during WWII. There were no airborne operations conducted by the USMC in WWII. Nobody bothered calling him on it as he'd just double down with an even bigger horseshit story.

Todd and his cousin had a major falling out with Joe Schons and his wife when the Schonses attempted to start a marijuana plant growing operation on their land, which was a challenging task, and the Schons managed to "screw it up in every possible way." A group of local thieves soon targeted the Schons' marijuana crop. The best way to access Schons' pot farm was to drive across part of Todd's cousin's property, and one day in 1978, Todd and his cousin spotted the thieves in a van driving across his cousin's property and heading away from the direction of the Schons' land. Todd and his cousin got in a truck and gave chase to the thieves.

Traveling at a high rate of speed and spitting gravel and dust behind their truck, Todd and his cousin caught up with the thieves on Berry Creek Road. The chase had caused the thieves' van to skid off the road and crash into some trees, totaling it. The impact of the crash resulted in all four occupants being injured. After making sure that the thieves did not have any life-threatening injuries, Todd and his cousin collected some guns that the thieves had in their van as "souvenirs."

Todd and his cousin then returned home and were met by Schons' wife, standing in the driveway, who was screaming at them and accusing them of stealing her cash crop of marijuana. Todd and his cousin then directed Ms. Schons to where the totaled van could be located with her "sh*tty product" inside. Later that day Todd and his cousin heard on the local six o'clock news (and in the newspaper the following day) that they were being sought by the police in connection to the van chase. Todd said that all the locals, "knew they did it, loved it, and no one gave them up."

As could be predicted, they were on the outs with the Schonses after that incident. The Schonses attempted to grow marijuana again the following year, but their effort was poorly concealed, and their loose lips resulted in their being raided by the Butte County Sheriff's office. Surprisingly, no arrests were made. That fact began to fuel some speculation among the locals that Schons may have been a police informant.

Another incident that stands out among many involving Schons, Todd, and Todd's cousin, was a time when Schons opened fire with a rifle from his property, uphill from Todd's cousin's place. One of the bullets hit a small building on the cousin's property, and several others hit the dirt, narrowly missing Todd's cousin's small children who were playing outside. Todd had quickly grabbed a gun in self-defense and had Schons in his gunsights, but his cousin talked him out of returning fire, possibly sparing Schon's life. Todd then ran to a neighbor's house. The neighbor had company at the time, and they all had witnessed the entire incident.

The Sheriff's department was called out, and even with many witnesses, Schons inexplicably was not arrested. This further fueled rumors that he was somehow connected to law enforcement, possibly even before he moved to Berry Creek, and was being protected by them.

Todd said that eventually Joe Schons "made so many enemies, that his stuck vehicles would be vandalized before they could be recovered. We saw his lifted pickup broken down on the way to town one day. It had no wheels on it when we came back up later that day, A few years after I moved out of state, I heard the locals succeeded in running the Schonses out of town, which had probably happened before, and again wherever they went."

According to Todd, none of the locals knew what Schons did for a living. He claimed that he was a substance abuse counselor, but neither he nor his wife were ever seen going to work.

When I asked Todd to give his honest opinion about whether Joe Schons could have been responsible for the disappearance of the Yuba County Five, he said that Schons' contention that he was checking the snowpack for a family weekend at a cabin, is "laughable." He added that Schons and his wife could barely exist in the same trailer together, let alone vacation together, and anything else that Schons told police was likely made up on the spot as the man was a "wet brain alcoholic and a pathological liar."

When I further pressed Todd on his thoughts on Schons being involved he said:

> A very strange thing about the incident is that Schons, or the 4 men, ended up 8 miles past Mountain House at 5:00 pm in February. You don't get from Oroville to there by accident, as you are ascending steep grades that can't go unnoticed. It's like driving up to the Overlook Hotel in movie *The Shining*. Mountain House, a small lodge owned by locals Roland & Suzanne, was the last outpost on the Oroville-Quincy hwy., was where the pavement ended, and desolate wilderness began. Schons was usually on roads closer to home, and by that late in the day, he would have been sloshed. People he didn't know would get him unstuck, unhook the chain, and he'd drive off, no thank you or conversation.

The final wildcard of all the theories of what may have befallen the Yuba County Five is the account of Joe Schons. His story of seeing the Boys the night of the basketball game appears never to have been deeply scrutinized. It was noted in many of the newspaper articles on the case that his story changed at least a few times. Law enforcement was also aware of this but appeared to accept Schons' excuse of being in pain from his heart attack and possibly hallucinating.

From newspaper reports, the only part of Schons' account that seems to have been corroborated is his suffering a heart attack. From what I have researched, it would have been impossible for doctors to know after the fact exactly when his heart attack happened. I do not know if the police ever bothered to verify that Schons indeed owned a cabin that far up the Oroville-Quincy Highway. Schons' story was that he was checking the snowpack around his cabin in advance of a ski weekend with his wife and daughter.

From my own research, I found that Schons' primary residence was on Raccoon Road, and he had property on the adjoining Schons' Drive in Berry Creek. This location is roughly an hour south of the Rogers Cow Camp area, where Jack Madruga's car was abandoned. I did find a record of Schons owning a property at 8805 Oroville-Quincy Highway in 1969, but this property is also about an hour south of where the car was abandoned. The physical address listed for the Rogers Cow Camp Campground is 16333 Oroville-Quincy Highway.

Other aspects of Schons' story should have been better scrutinized by law enforcement. He claimed that despite having a heart attack, he was able to walk (at least a few miles) back to the Mountain House Lodge after his VW Beetle had run out of gas.

It is also odd that Schons claimed to stay in his stationary car with the heater running to stay warm. As I mentioned earlier, the Volkswagen Beetle does not produce any heat when the car is not moving. As stated on the BugShop website "Keep in mind that the volume of hot air that is blown into the car is dependent on the fan in the fan shroud, which is dependent on the engine RPM."

Other than keeping the cold wind off him, the inside of the Schons Beetle would have been terribly cold that night. Being a local, why would he not have attempted to make the trek back to the Mountain House Lodge sooner?

There is another aspect of Schons' story that does not seem to add up. He clearly stated that at two different times during the night, he saw people on the road, outside of their car, and he called out to them for help, and they did not respond. From all accounts of the families of the Boys, the Boys would not ever ignore anyone's calls for help. If the Boys were not able to help Schons because they were under the control of another person or persons, why would the other people not make sure that Schons did not get a good look at them, especially if they were in the process of committing a crime or had already committed a crime against Gary?

When I asked Todd, who knew Joe Schons from Berry Creek, if he believed that Schons' story was plausible, he told me the following:

> The Oroville-Quincy Highway was a state-maintained road, and even the dirt portion of it was quite broad and flat. However, all bets were off in the winter months, when frequent heavy rains could badly damage any road, any time. Years ago, they started closing that road in the winter, due to washouts. Driving a passenger car would be no problem, but conditions could change rapidly into a 4WD-only situation. It's hard to say what that road was like, eight miles past Mountain House, on that day.
>
> They could have followed Schons, but it's more likely that he got stuck earlier in the day and was unable to free his vehicle. Schons would have leapt at the chance to inject himself into the goings on, and his "scouting out a camping spot" story was just the tip of the bullshit iceberg, no doubt. The rest of his account

sounds exactly like the kind of nonsense he was known to fabricate, out of thin air, and for no reason. There's a good chance he didn't remember anything that transpired, or that he pieced it together, after hearing about the incident.

My cousin and his wife feel that Schons had a hand in what happened to those five men, but we'll likely never know exactly what took place. Would an idiot like Schons send them off in the wrong direction? You bet he would.

At best, he misdirected the investigation, and at worst, he caused these men's demise.

I found out on my own a very interesting fact about Joe Schons: his 18-year-old (in 1978) daughter had a cognitive disability called dysphasia. Dysphasia is a condition that affects a person's ability to produce and understand spoken language. Dysphasia can also cause reading, writing, and gesturing impairments. Schons' daughter is one of a small group of developmentally disabled adults in the "North State" who actually vote.
(https://www.newsreview.com/chico/growing-group-of-voters/content?oid=2346285)

I found this fact to be very intriguing as it opens the possibility that Schons and his daughter could have crossed paths with one or more of the Boys through the Gateway Projects or events for the disabled. It was reported in several newspaper accounts, including the article in the June 14, 1978 *Napa Valley Register*, that the Boys "attended dances for the handicapped in Sacramento." Could Shons' daughter have been at one of these dances? It must also be considered a possibility that Schons' daughter could have been involved with a program at the Gateway Projects, where the Boys were a fixture.

It should also be mentioned that Todd reported that Joe Schons claimed to be a drug abuse counselor. The Gateway Projects also offered drug abuse counseling, which is why Gary Mathias went to Gateway and subsequently became involved with the Gateway Gators basketball team.

A final word about Schons from Todd:

> People told me various tales of their run-ins with Joe and/or Cindy Schons, but most of them gravitated towards drunken buffoonery and callous disregard. My memory of what I experienced firsthand is sharp, but fuzzy for anything I heard from others. There were only a couple of local watering holes - The Sugar Pine, Mountain House and a little bar in Brush Creek - and Joe pretty much wore out his welcome in all of them, in short order. There was quite a mix of characters around back then - loggers, Native Americans, tradesmen, hippies, survivalists, growers, veterans - and most of us were a combination of the aforementioned. I stayed out of the bars, after almost catching a stray bullet in a parking lot, during a brawl. The sheriffs were 40 minutes away, in Oroville.

> One common thread with the Schons family was malicious gossip, which originated with them. They got themselves in trouble multiple times over that. Another was stiffing people they hired, for work that was done at their place. That pissed off a lot of people. When it came to maintaining the road we all used, which disappeared yearly, we and our good neighbors toiled and spent thousands, with nothing but blabbering contributed by the Schons. Toss in Joe's vehicular misadventures, which were many, and you've pretty much got the picture, which was more miserable than interesting.

> Did Joe sometimes get a kick in the ass or a punch in the

face? Yes, he did. Now if the Schonses turned up dead, you'd have the makings of a good who-done-it because there'd be 50 suspects with a motive. I loved living up there and have a lot of good memories of my years in Berry Creek.

It takes all kinds to make a world, I guess.

God help us all.

CHAPTER 9: FINAL THOUGHTS

Over the years, there have been quite a few theories, some more outlandish than others, of what could have led the Yuba County Boys to their heart-breaking fate. One sparsely subscribed to theory links the Boys' disappearance to a series of arson attacks on the Gateway Projects facility and its director.

On February 18th, 1975, three years before the Boys disappeared, an arsonist burned to the ground a Gateway Projects workshop building in Yuba City. Two weeks later, on March 1st, a Molotov cocktail was thrown through a broken window of the main Gateway Projects office. Only minor damage was inflicted in that particular case. Seven weeks after the workshop was burned down, Gateway Projects Director, 42-year-old Donald Garrett, was burned alive when the apartment building in which he lived was set ablaze. Local police detected the strong odor of a flammable liquid when they entered Garrett's apartment. A rag was also found at the top of a staircase by the apartment.

WORKSHOP ACTIVITY—Gateway Projects Executive Director Don Garrett (left photo, in white shirt) and Production Manager Hugh Allen discuss program progress at the Franklin Avenue workshop, where Pacific Gas and Electric equipment is prepared for shipment. Shop

Gateway Projects Executive Director Don Garrett
Marysville Appeal Democrat, Marysville,
California, August 17, 1974, page 14

No arrests were ever made in the arson cases. The Yuba County Sheriff's Department did not believe that the attacks on Gateway and its director were connected to the Boy's disappearance, but as there were never any suspects, a possible connection cannot be ruled out.

Man Dies In Yuba City Fire; Police Probe Arson

McClatchy Newspaper Service

YUBA CITY — The director of a Yuba City program for the handicapped, Donald D. Garrett, burned to death in a fire in his apartment last night, seven weeks after an arson-caused blaze leveled a program workshop building.

Garrett, 42, of Gateway Projects Inc., was pronounced dead at his residence at the Sugar House Apartments at about 8:30 p.m.

Police Lt. Robert Smith said officers detected an odor of flammable liquid when they entered the apart-ment. He also said a rag was found at that time he also said there was a possibility that the fire at his workship and attempted fire at the main office might have been related to the others.

Authorities said the exact cause of Garrett's death was pending until an autopsy can be performed.

Yuba City financier Daryl Morrison, who owns the apartment complex, was visibly upset by the fire, pushing reporters as they attempted to question and photograph deputies removing the body from the building.

The Sacramento Bee, April 7, 1975, Page 5

One of the fringe theories of what happened to the Yuba County Five blames some sort of supernatural force for leading the Boys up the cold mountain. This case is sometimes referred to as America's Dyatlov Pass. This is a reference to the Dyatlov Pass Incident, a mysterious event in which nine Russian hikers disappeared from their camp in Russia's Ural Mountains in February 1959.

During the night, something caused the hikers, who were inadequately dressed for the heavy snowfall and subzero temperatures, to cut their way out of their tent and flee the campsite.

The bodies of the hikers were eventually found in the snow with many of the bodies showing strange injuries. One man had a fractured skull. Two of the hikers had fractured chest injuries. One hiker was missing both eyes, and one was missing her tongue. The incident was investigated by Russian Authorities, who determined that a compelling natural force had caused the deaths. Like the case of The Yuba County Five, there are many theories on what happened to the Russian hikers, but none of the theories have been proven. Also like the Yuba case, many reports of the Dyatlov incident contradict other reports.

Some online theorists believe that both of the incidents may have been the result of some sort of paranormal phenomenon, such as a UFO or a Sasquatch, causing the groups to flee in a panic.

Like many of the family members of the Yuba County Five, I believe someone, or something, scared the Boys up that mountain. If they were simply looking for help, why did they go uphill? Jack Madruga and Gary Mathias would have known how to get the others to push Jack's car and free it if it had been stuck in the snow. All paranormal explanations aside, it would make the most sense that someone threatened the Boys, possibly firing a gun into the air, making them go up the cold mountain. This possibility would explain why some believe gun shell casings were found very close to where Jack's car was abandoned.

If the Boys were told to go up the mountain at gunpoint, then who ordered them to do so? Could Joe Schons be telling the truth for the most part? If so, it makes the story of an altercation taking place at either Behr's Market or on the Oroville Dam bridge seem far more plausible. Could Joe Schons' sighting of a second vehicle, possibly a red truck parked behind Jack's Montego, explain how the Boys may have been followed up Oroville-Quincy Highway? Could the Boys have been following the second vehicle until they got the Montego stuck in the snow? Were they then ordered out of Jack's car and forced to go up the mountain?

Could Alan Martin be telling the truth about Gary Mathias' murder? Was Gary thrown over the Oroville Dam during an altercation with someone he knew? Did the four remaining Boys witness Gary's murder? Did Alan Martin order the four remaining Boys into Jack's car and drive them up the hill, only to force them to scramble for their lives partway to the summit? Were the four remaining Boys told to follow someone until they reached Rogers Cow Camp, at which point they were forced to flee up the mountain?

This theory does not explain how Gary's shoes ended up in the trailer, but it does explain why the remains of Gary Mathias were never found. It would also explain why no one built a fire at the Forest Service trailer.

It should also be considered that the reports of the Behr's Market parking lot brawl, which some family members believe occurred, could have been misreports of the Oroville Dam bridge brawl. Or vice versa. Many "reports" in the Yuba County Five case are little more than persistent rumors, repeated and speculated on over the decades.

We may never know why the Boys of the Yuba County Five, clad only in street clothes, left their perfectly running car to head uphill in freezing temperatures and high snowdrifts, but after my own investigation of this case, I believe some very likely assumptions can be made. In my opinion, one of the strongest assumptions is that Jack Madruga drove his own car up the mountain to where it was abandoned near Rogers Cow Camp. I base this on the investigators' reports of no damage to the undercarriage of Jack's Mercury Montego. Investigators believed that for the car's undercarriage to have so little damage, the driver must have been familiar with driving on the Oroville-Quincy Highway, especially at night.

The families stated that none of the Boys had been familiar with that part of the Oroville-Quincy Highway. I believe investigators missed just how meticulous Jack Madruga was in caring for his car. He wanted the underside of his Montego, even though no one would ever see it, to look as good as the parts of his car that everyone could see. Jack's nephew George Madruga really stressed to me that if Jack were unfamiliar with a road that he thought would damage his car, he would flat-out refuse to drive on it. If Jack did have to go down a road that looked questionable to him, he would drive very carefully and avoid any ruts or obvious potholes.

If someone other than Jack, even if that someone knew the area and the road, had driven Jack's car up the mountain on the night of February 24, 1978, he would not have been as careful a driver as Jack would have been. A driver other than Jack would have had no incentive to drive with extreme caution to avoid ruts or other obstacles that could damage the car. In my opinion, the good condition of the Montego's undercarriage could only result from Jack's having driven the car on that rutted gravel road. Further supporting the theory that Jack drove the Montego is the fact that Jack's car keys were in his pocket when his body was recovered.

There will always be suspicion that Gary Mathias was somehow responsible for the tragedy that occurred to his friends, but there is no physical evidence that supports this suspicion. Someone must have taken care of Ted Weiher for the weeks that he survived in the Forest Service trailer. Jackie, Jack, and Bill would not have been capable of doing that. With the authorities believing that Jack Madruga and Bill Sterling had succumbed to the elements before they could make it to the Forest Service trailer, only Jackie Huett would be left to care for Ted if Gary were not there. Jackie was not able to care for himself and would not have been able to take care of someone else.

Jack Madruga's niece Cathy did tell me that it was no secret that the Boys were afraid of Gary and what he might do. She added that they did not want Gary to go to the game with them, but they were too scared to tell him that he could not go.

The strange past of Gary Mathias and the credible sighting of him by Cathy Madruga Roberts after the Boys' disappearance lead me to strongly consider that Gary made it to the trailer, swapped shoes with Ted Weiher, headed out into the cold woods, and somehow made it out of the mountains. Could Gary Mathias still be out there somewhere and being off of his medication, not know who he is? Could he be among the many homeless people in California, Oregon, or Washington? It's also likely that Gary made it just far enough from the trailer that his remains were never found after he succumbed to the elements.

The theory that boys simply got lost (often called "The Wrong Turn Theory") is still frequently discussed on websites like Redditt. This theory would indeed be the most plausible way to explain why the boys got off course: taking a wrong turn in the dark, possibly on their way to Forbestown for Gary to visit his friends. Because it was stressed to me by Jack Madruga's nephew, George Madruga, that Jack absolutely knew how to turn around his car when lost, I simply do not buy into that theory. I feel that the boys had some sort of reason to go up the mountain. Either they were told to follow someone under threat, or they were in the process of fleeing from someone.

I have also read that some believe that carbon monoxide may have leaked inside Jack's car, causing him and the other boys to be light-headed and start becoming ill. That theory would suggest that when Jack's car got stuck in the snow, the tail pipe became covered, and carbon monoxide backed up into the car. That would still not answer the million-dollar question: why did the boys go up the road in the first place?

Secondly, if the boys had become sick or dizzy, why would they feel the need to leave their car, particularly in light of the fact that people who don't feel well would probably not want to hike up hill in deep snowdrifts? If Jack Madruga did drive his own car up the road, it is still hard to explain why he would have left it with the driver's side window partially rolled down if he had not planned on coming back to the car. That is something Jack Madruga simply would never do unless he was under duress.

I have also seen it suggested online that it was possible that Jack's car stalled out when it was stuck in the snow and that he "flooded it out" trying to restart it. I do believe that may have happened as older cars without modern fuel injection systems can stall out in cold temperatures.

I was working on my personal theory that the boys somehow ran into Joe Schons and decided to help him get his VW Bug unstuck from the snow somewhere closer to their path home (near Oroville) and wound up following him further north up the Oroville-Quincy Highway, where Schons may have gotten out of his VW Bug and made Jack roll his window down to talk to him. Then Schons may have pulled out a gun and forced the boys out of the car and up the mountain. But this, like so many of the other theories in this baffling case, is like building a Jenga puzzle. As soon as you make a foundation and add to it, it all comes crumbling down.

An intriguing theory has been proposed by a message board poster called earlraul. Basing his theory on his understanding that there were witnesses to Joe Schons' having a drink in the Mountain House Lodge, earlraul speculates that Schons may have stopped at the Mountain House after he had gone up the mountain (not on his way up the mountain, as Shons claimed) and had a run-in with the Boys. In order to establish an alibi, Shons walked down to the Mountain House Lodge, told people at the Lodge that he was on his way up the mountain, then walked back to his car and waited until morning to walk back for help.

There are still many unanswered questions in this baffling case. The known facts of this incident have not changed since 1978. Gary Mathias is still missing and unaccounted for. Ted Weiher lived for some time after the Boys went missing, and someone took care of him for at least some of the time that he was in the trailer. Gary Mathias' shoes were found in the Forest Service Trailer. Four of the Boys sadly died from exposure to the freezing conditions in the mountains.

The only fact that has come into greater focus after the incident was the turbulent and sometimes violent past of Gary Mathias. This was mostly due to the 2019 article in *The Sacramento Bee* Newspaper.

As mentioned previously, family members of the Yuba County Five have speculated about what may have caused the Boys to go missing:

    a. a "brawl" at Behr's Market

    b. a fight on the Oroville Dam bridge that resulted in Gary Mathias' murder, with his body thrown into the water and never recovered.

    c. Gary's being targeted by someone who knew him, resulting in his being thrown over the dam, possibly by a man who later became a pastor.

    d. The highly speculated theory of Gary Mathias' being responsible for the deaths of the other Boys, either directly or indirectly.

    e. Lastly, my personal theory that Joe Schons could have been solely responsible for the deaths of the Boys, either intentionally or unintentionally, by pointing them in the wrong direction, possibly under the guise of sending them into the mountains to get help for him or someone else.

We may never which of these theories (or a combination thereof) is correct.

What we do know is that a horrendous tragedy occurred to five men in their prime. It not only deprived them of their lives but also deprived their families of ever seeing them again. We can only hope that death came quickly and painlessly for Jack, Jackie, and Bill. We can also hope that someone gave comfort to Ted Weiher in his agonizing last days. Finally, we can hope that Gary somehow made it out of the frozen woods and will one day be found and remember what happened on that tragic night back in February

1978.

Do not judge a biography by its length
Nor by the number of pages in it
Judge it by the richness of its contents

Sometimes those unfinished are among the most poignant

Do not judge a song by its duration
Nor by the number of its notes
Judge it by the way it touches and lifts the soul

Sometimes those unfinished are among the most beautiful

And when something has enriched your life
And when its melody lingers on in your heart

Is it unfinished?
Or is it endless?

- Anonymous

BIBLIOGRAPHY

Egel, Benjy, "Out in the Cold: Were 4 mentally disabled men set up to die in the California woods?" *The Sacramento Bee*, February 26, 2019. Yuba County 5: Who was Gary Mathias, where did he disappear to? | The Sacramento Bee (sacbee.com)

Foul Play Suspected in Disappearance of 5, *The Los Angeles Times*, March 10, 1978

Gorney, Cynthia, 5 'Boys' Who Never Come Back, The Washington Post, July 6, 1978
5 'Boys' Who Never Come Back - The Washington Post

"Let's Talk about It: Gary Mathias and Four Friends," The Charley Project Blog
Let's talk about it: Gary Mathias and his four friends – The Charley Project Blog (wordpress.com)

Marysville Appeal Democrat, Marysville, California, August 17, 1974

Marysville Appeal Democrat, Marysville, CA, March 2, 1978, Page 8 https://newspaperarchive.com/advertisement-clipping-mar-02-1978-1958313/

Marysville Appeal Democrat, Marysville, CA, February 24, 1979

Napa Valley Register, Napa, CA, June 13, 1978

Nelthropp, Chelsea, What Happened to the Yuba County Five?

Vocal
What Happened to the Yuba County Five? (vocal.media)

Pacific Daily News, Agana Heights, Guam, August 6, 1978, page 16

Rossen, Jake, 'Bizarre as Hell': The Disappearance of the Yuba County Five, *Mental Floss*, March 16, 2018
'Bizarre as Hell': The Disappearance of the Yuba County Five | Mental Floss

The Hanford Sentinel, Hanford, CA June 13, 1978, p. 14

The Haunting Case of the Mathias Group (Yuba County Five) *Strange Outdoors* Dec. 8, 2017
The haunting case of the Mathias Group (Yuba County Five) — StrangeOutdoors.com

The Los Angeles Times, March 10, 1978

The New York Daily News, New York, NY, Jan. 7, 1979

The Sacramento Bee, April 7, 1975, p. 5

The Washington Post, Washington, D.C., July 6, 1978

"Yuba County Five: An Overview," *Astonishing Legends* https://www.astonishinglegends.com/astonishing-legends/2020/10/24/yuba-county-five-an-overview

ACKNOWLEDGEMENT

I would like to give a huge thank you to my brilliant editor, Deneen Shreve, whose advice and encouragement have been invaluable to me in the writing of this book.

ABOUT THE AUTHOR

Drew Hurst Beeson

Drew Hurst Beeson has been exploring the unknown all of his life. Out of Bounds: What Happened to the Yuba County Five? is his third book about American unsolved crimes. He is the author of Paratrooper of Fortune: The Story of Ted B. Braden - Vietnam Commando, CIA Operative, Congo Mercenary, and just maybe D.B. Cooper, Sighting In on The Zodiac Killer:

Unmasking America's Most Puzzling Unsolved Murders, The Cloak of the Brethren, and Asleep in Hell.

Drew had recently been featured on a number of radio shows and podcasts, including Coast to Coast AM with George Noory, House of Mystery with Al Warren and Michael Butterfield, The Cooper Vortex with Darren Schaeffer, Paranormal Dimensions with David Young, Conspiracy Unlimited with Richard Syrett, and HyperSpace with Solaris BlueRaven.

Drew is the host of two podcasts and a YouTube channel. Please join him for fascinating discussions on unsolved crime, perplexing mysteries, and the paranormal.

"Drew Crime" podcast on Podbean
"The Zodcast" on Podbean

Drew's YouTube channel is named "Drew Beeson"
https://www.youtube.com/channel/
UCxv5Efss01iDhELoBZwdDw

BOOKS BY THIS AUTHOR

Paratrooper Of Fortune: The Story Of Ted B. Braden - Vietnam Commando, C. I. A. Operative, Congo Mercenary, And Just Maybe D. B. Cooper

Ted B. Braden was "the perfect combination of high intelligence and criminality." - Jo Ann, Ted Braden's sister-in-law

November 24th, 2021 will mark the 50th Anniversary of the only unsolved skyjacking case in American history. The case, nicknamed "Norjack" by the FBI as it involved the hijacking of a Northwest Orient 727 Airliner, would create a folk hero, if not a legend, of a mysterious man who would be immortalized by the name D.B. Cooper.

This fascinating case has garnered a myriad of colorful and interesting suspects. One of the "dark horse" suspects who emerged over the years was a member of the most elite Special Forces unit created by the United States Government to serve during the war in Vietnam: a secret and covert unit called the Military Assistance Command, Vietnam – Studies and Observations Group (MACV-SOG). This rather benign-sounding name served as a thin veil, masking what was known to a few as the "black ops" unit in Vietnam.

Many of the soldiers who served in this elite unit consider one of their own to be the infamous D.B. Cooper who hijacked Northwest Orient Flight 305; demanded a ransom of $200,000 in cash; and jumped out of the lowered aft staircase of the plane into the stormy night, never to be seen again. It was even stated by some of the most highly-decorated members of MACV-SOG, legends such as Major John Plaster and Sergeant Billy Waugh, that one man in SOG had the parachuting expertise, the know-how, and, most of all, the "balls of steel" to pull off the D.B. Cooper skyjacking.

This man was Ted B. Braden.

Raised in the Mid-West during the Great Depression, young Ted could not have foreseen that the trajectory of his life would be set by events happening thousands of miles from his boyhood home. At age 16, Braden joined the army to fight in World War II, a decision that led to a twenty-year on-again/off-again military career marked by dangerous covert operations; C.I.A. intrigue; desertion, arrest, and incarceration (only for him to be freed without trial under mysterious circumstances); Cold War mercenarism; and ultimately, distrust in a government for whom he could have surrendered his life.

The story of Ted B. Braden, master parachutist and soldier of fortune, trained by Uncle Sam in the art of war but not in the art of peace, is the quintessential American story, the story of the men of his generation and of a war that defined that generation.

Ted Braden was an enigma as a person, driven by a brilliant, unorthodox mind that struggled to adapt to a society based on law and order and routine. He was a true super soldier who was suspected of having mental illness, most likely from post-traumatic stress disorder. He was a tortured soul with the burning frustration that he could never parlay his soldiering skills into big financial gains. He was fearless in his military endeavors to the point of risking lives but was endowed with natural instincts of survival that kept him and the men under his command alive.

It is tragic that a man like this is no longer alive to share his story.

It is tragic that a man like this never will be fully understood. He had an ability to be very kind and very cruel, an ability to be very forthright and very cunning, an ability to be very committed as a soldier and very adrift as a civilian.

Was he the man who fearlessly leapt out of a Boeing 727 with $200,000 strapped around his body on a rainy Thanksgiving Eve in 1971? We may never know, but even if Ted Braden is not D.B. Cooper, he is one of the most fascinating people whose story you never knew - until now.

Sighting In On The Zodiac Killer: Unmasking America's Most Puzzling Unsolved Murders

Now updated with compelling new information!
December 20, 2019, marked the 51st anniversary of the first canonical Zodiac crime, and for decades, police and amateur detectives have been searching for clues to the identity of the man whose reign of terror began the year after the "Summer of Love."

After 50 years is it possible for anyone to discover anything new, anything that will unmask the infamous killer? Drew Hurst Beeson says, "Yes," and in Sighting In on The Zodiac Killer, he reveals the newly-discovered clues, the fascinating connections, and the compelling evidence that point to the man, hiding in plain sight, who just might be the Zodiac Killer.

The Cloak Of The Brethren

Blue Monday. 9-to-5. Gray flannel suit. Starbucks. Dean Braden, property manager, had settled into the routine of a comfortable life until an unusual request from his boss propels him into a swirling vortex of murder and mystery, which leads him on a search for the truth and has him running for his life.

Asleep In Hell

Can an antique bed be a portal to another realm? Asleep in Hell explores this possibility. Join us on a true-life journey into one of the great mysteries of the universe. Asleep is Hell is the story of a young man and his cousin who use their grandfather's old iron bed to furnish a bedroom of their apartment - with unexpected and terrifying results!

Printed in Great Britain
by Amazon

81457408R00088